ELUSIVE RUSSIA
Current Developments in Russian State Identity
and Institutional Reform under President Putin

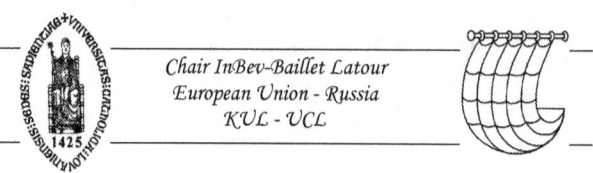

CHAIR INBEV-BAILLET LATOUR "EUROPEAN UNION – RUSSIA"

Created in 2000, the main objective of the Chair InBev-Baillet Latour is to encourage multidisciplinary research on the relations between the European Union and Russia. The Chair InBev – Baillet Latour is based on a cooperation between the *Institut d'Études européennes* of Université Catholique de Louvain and the *Instituut voor Internationaal en Europees Beleid* of Katholieke Universiteit Leuven. The research primarily focuses on the analysis of the origins, determinants and possible evolutions of EU-Russia relations. The Chair aims to create a dialogue between a broad group of people sharing an interest in EU – Russia relations: students, academics, diplomats, policy makers and business people are invited to share their views and knowledge in the seminars, conferences and publications organized by the Chair InBev - Baillet Latour.

In addition to book volumes, the Chair InBev – Baillet Latour also publishes a Working Papers Series. The Working Papers as well as information on the Chair's activities at K.U.Leuven are available at http://www.iieb.be/ibl

Katlijn Malfliet and Ria Laenen (eds)

Elusive Russia

CURRENT DEVELOPMENTS IN RUSSIAN STATE IDENTITY
AND INSTITUTIONAL REFORM UNDER PRESIDENT PUTIN

LEUVEN UNIVERSITY PRESS
2007

© 2007 by Leuven University Press / Presses Universitaires de Louvain / Universitaire Pers Leuven. Minderbroedersstraat 4, B-3000 Leuven (Belgium)

All rights reserved. Except in those cases expressly determined by law, no part of this publication may be multiplied, saved in an automated datafile or made public in any way whatsoever without the express prior written consent of the publishers.

ISBN 978 90 5867 608 5
D / 2007 / 1869 / 28

NUR: 754

TABLE OF CONTENTS

Preface   7
Katlijn Malfliet and Ria Laenen

Authority and Identity in Russia   13
Marie Mendras

Russian Nationalism under Putin: A Majority Faith?   33
Luke March

The Outcomes of a Decade of Federal Reforms   53
in Russia and the Newest Developments
Irina Busygina

The Russian Parliament and the Presidency of Vladimir Putin   73
Andrei Zakharov

Conclusions   85
Katlijn Malfliet and Ria Laenen

About the Authors   89

LIST OF ABBREVIATIONS

CIS	Commonwealth of Independent States
IMF	International Monetary Fund
KhMAD	Khanti-Mansi Autonomous District
KPAD	Komi-Permyak Autonomous District
KPRF	Communist Party of the Russian Federation (Kommunisticheskaya partiya Rossiiskoi Federatsii)
LDPR	Liberal Democratic Party of Russia (Liberal'no-demokraticheskaya partiya Rossii)
NATO	North Atlantic Treaty Organization
NBP	National Bolshevik Party (Natsional-bol'shevistskaya partiya)
NNP	People's National Party
PCA	Partnership and Cooperation Agreement
RNE	Russian National Unity (Russkoe natsional'noe edinstvo)
RSFSR	Russian Socialist Federated Soviet Republic
SPS	Union of Rightist Forces
UN	United Nations
USSR	Union of Soviet Socialist Republics
YaNAD	Yamalo-Nenetz Autonomous District

PREFACE

Katlijn Malfliet and Ria Laenen

Today we find ourselves in the middle of a vigorous debate on the ontology of the Russian state. Is Russia gradually developing towards a democratic state organization and can we conclude, as Andrei Shleifer does in his latest book, that Russia is a "normal" half-developed democracy?[1] Or should we speak about a "Potemkin democracy" and did Russia become a unique laboratory for what Andrew Wilson calls "virtual politics"?[2] Western as well as Russian experts largely disagree on this subject; the two camps drew their swords in this discussion although probably both sides are entitled to a part of the truth.

Harvard economist Andrei Shleifer is a confirmed believer in the thesis that Russia can be compared to developing countries such as Mexico, Brazil, Croatia or Malaysia: typical middle-income countries with an unfinished democracy and a stumbling market economy. He brings the controversial argument that a decade after communism, Russia had become a normal country: a democratic market economy, albeit, admittedly, a highly imperfect one. Shleifer, who was an adviser to the Russian government in the 1990s, sees the shock therapy of the early nineties as rather healthy for the country, as it needed a radical deconstruction of the communist state-party system and a depoliticization of the economy. In what became a classical debate between economists - the choice between shock therapy and more gradual step by step changes- Shleifer believes that slow state controlled reforms would have been much more pricy than radical and thorough changes. In this light, the Yeltsin period is seen as period of necessary reforms in the first decade after the collapse of the Soviet Union. The impression of chaos, miserable social conditions, self-enrichment and the strange phenomenon of the "Family" should be considered, according to Shleifer, as a matter of folklore, which is accompanying these badly needed radical reforms. The rise of the class of Oligarchs that came to power is for Shleifer an almost natural phenomenon that can be observed in many countries in that stage of

---

[1] Shleifer Andrei, *A Normal Country. Russia after Communism*, Harvard University Press, 2005.
[2] Wilson Andrew, *Virtual Politics. Faking Democracy in the Post-Soviet World*, Yale University Press, 2005.

development. Russia is not extremely corrupt or repressive, he argues, when you compare it to presidential democracies as Brazil or Argentina.

We understand that Shleifer wants to be provocative in his book, when he tries to counter the widespread belief that ill-advised government policies, especially the policy of privatization, led to economic decline, and allowed for the rise of the Oligarchs. Perhaps, he should be more cautious in defending such a thesis given all the failures of the shock therapies that were introduced on Western advice in post-communist countries. In the 1990s Russia witnessed an increase in income inequality, a sharp drop in life expectancy, the 1998 financial crisis,.... Liberal economists saw unhindered privatizations as a triumph of their belief in a restricted role of the state, be it in a command economy or in a Western welfare state. Liberal economists are missing part of the picture, and this reduction is not innocent.

Andrew Wilson, on the contrary, sees Russia's unique political order as a typical example of post-communist "virtual politics". As a political scientist, he looks at reforms with a much more critical eye. According to him, political parties are created, bought, frustrated or suppressed by the power; elections are orchestrated; information is controlled and manipulated: formal democracy is manipulated. Democracy becomes political technology, managed by the insider elite. Putin is a "persona" (with the Greek connotation of "mask"), created by the Yeltsin Family. However, it soon became clear that Vladimir Putin had higher ambitions than being a puppet in the hands of his predecessor and he became the main manager himself, firmly taking control over the "managed democracy" of Russia. In the running up period to the December 2007 parliamentary elections and the 2008 presidential elections, the managed character of the electoral democracy is again being confirmed. As a result of the new electoral legislation that came into force on January 1, 2007 the number of political parties will be significantly reduced. The law is clearly aimed at disabling any potential opposition to the pro-Kremlin party "United Russia" that currently dominates the Duma. There even has been created a "managed" opposition party called "A Just Russia", since having some opposition forces is regarded as a requirement to qualify as a democracy. So, continuous efforts are being made to keep the façade of democracy intact. Although Russian policy makers master the language of democracy fluently, serious questions can be raised about the degree in which they truly believe in the need for a democratic process of government.

Again, we experience difficulties in categorizing Russia in the classical concepts of political science. Russia experts McFaul, Petrov and Ryabov caught this difficulty of categorizing Russia by describing it as being "between dictatorship and democracy".[3] Again, we can observe a radicalization of the extreme approaches in thinking about Russia. Indeed, why is it so difficult to accept Russia as a state with its own peculiarities? How is it possible that the uneasiness and divide on Russia is still omnipresent? The theme of Russian exceptionalism is a card that often has been played by specialists from Russia themselves, as well as by the area specialists. In this respect, the younger generation of Russian scholars' efforts to analyze the case of Russia in a comparative framework applying theories of International Relations or economic studies –as Shleifer does - are an encouraging sign that the gap between area studies and the field of political sciences is narrowing. Nevertheless, the uneasiness in dealing with Russia remains. Partly, this problem can be attributed to the mixed signals being given by post-Soviet Russia itself. The clichéd Russian identity crisis has not yet been solved. Russia is still in search of its own place in the world. In this search domestic and foreign policy issues are closely intertwined.

The outcome of Russia's state and nation building project is not without relevance for the international community's, and more specifically for the EU's relationship with Russia. In 1996 a series of American statements on Russia, both from policy makers and scholars, and most notably, Putin's speech at the Munich conference on Transatlantic Security on February 10, 2007 has led some observers to conclude that a reheating of the Cold War is taking place.[4] The EU's stance on Russia has been less outspoken critical. German Chancellor Angela Merkel has been raising human rights issues in talks with Putin and has been overall more vocal in voicing her concerns about Russia than her predecessor Schröder. Under Germany's current presidency of both the EU and the G8 there might be set a different tone in EU-Russia relations. In spite of the repeated confirmations that Russia is a strategic partner for the EU, it has become clear that a sense of

---

[3] Michael McFaul, N. Petrov and A. Ryabov, *Between Dictatorship and Democracy: Russian Post-Communist Political Reform*, Carnegie Endowment for International Peace: 2004.
[4] See, for instance, Council of Foreign Relations Report "Russia's Wrong Direction: What the United States Can and Should Do", March 2006, 94p.; Lieven Anatol, "Why are we trying to reheat the Cold War", *Los Angeles Times*, 18 March 2006; "No Cold War, Perhaps, but Surely a Lukewarm Peace", *NY Times*, 18 February 2007.

disillusionment is casting its shadow over EU – Russia relations. Indicative of this development is the fact that no breakthrough has yet been achieved on a new comprehensive agreement that should replace the current PCA that runs out in 2007. Russia's energy policy has emerged as a major obstacle in EU – Russia relations with Russia still refusing to ratify the EU's Energy Charter. Should the EU see today's Russia as an ally or as an adversary? It makes a difference whether we face a dictatorship or a democracy, whether we should consider Putin as a friendly head of state or as the one who demolishes the foundations of Russian democracy and who disrespects human rights. A recently released report by the Commission for the Protection of Journalists calls Putin "an elected leader who uses laws to control, intimidate, and censor the media".[5] In this regard, the discussion on the concept of "the dictatorship of the law" is interesting: can this mantra of Putin's policy approach be framed into Russia's own interpretation of the Rule of Law, or are we facing an unacceptable *contradictio in terminis*?

This book is based on the premise that Russian state identity and authority have a *sui generis* character. Attention is being paid to the historical background, such as the historic development of the role of the state in Russia, and other area specific elements (e.g. the sheer size of the Russian Federation) that make the case of Russia unique. After more than a decade and half, it seems that it is no longer adequate to put Russia in the category of "transition countries". People seem to need a black or white answer: has Russia become a fully fledged democracy or has it reverted to being an authoritarian state? Is it a developing country or a powerful global player? Are Russia's attempts to assert itself as a great power pure rhetoric by a state that is in fact weak or has Russia indeed regained great power status? Has the central state re-emerged as the most powerful player in Russian politics or have Russia's regions established themselves as bases for democratization in the federation?

The authors of this book do not come up with definitive answers to these questions. Instead, they provide us with a more nuanced view recognizing the achievements that have been made in the post-Soviet era, as well as highlighting some problematic developments observable in today's Russia. In this regard, the fact that the volume brings together contributions both from within and from outside Russia allows us to paint a balanced picture. Overall, the authors would agree that Russia is neither black nor white, but still in a state of flux. In other words, Russia to a large extent escapes our Western framework of thinking and, hence remains elusive.

---

[5] CPJ Report "Attacks on the Press in 2006" released on February 5, 2007.

This volume, which can be considered as a *status questionis* on current developments in Russia, brings together the views of four leading Russia experts on Russian state identity and institutional reform. Each of them shares with us his/her own original approach on some key components of today's Russian politics.

Marie Mendras sheds light on an underestimated aspect of the Russian polity: the bureaucracy that she interestingly depicts as an element of continuity and stability throughout different transition times. In her article she also addresses the age-old and still pressing question of Russia's relationship with its most significant "Other", i.e. Europe, a debate in which it is important to stress the distinction between Europe and the West. If Europe indeed is Russia's "preferred Other", as posed by Mendras, this offers both a promising as well as daunting perspective for the future development of EU – Russia relations.

Luke March highlights Russian nationalism as *the* story of contemporary Russian politics. He starts from the paradox that although Putin's regime has demonstrated ostensibly "nationalistic" features both domestically and internationally, it is precisely the absence of mass ethnic mobilization, electoral success for ethno-political parties, widespread ethnic unrest and revanchist foreign policy throughout the 1990s, that is most striking on a closer view. He emphasizes the importance of the imperial legacy, which hampered the emergence of both civic and ethnic nationalism, weak mass-elite linkages that have prevented mobilization of ethno-nationalist ideas. Most interesting is what he understands by effective management of nationalist sentiments by the political elite. Russian nationalism, he concludes, is by no means the majority faith of ethnic Russians today, but he sees indications under Putin that it remains a potent potential issue, and may be increasing in significance again.

Irina Busygina analyses how federalism has developed over the years since the first basic documents regulating Russia's federal relations were adopted in 1993. Putin's reforms have introduced a new type of center-periphery relations, new institutions have been created, while others have changed their role. Is this a "new" federation with a more centralized character and a drastically changed role of the regional elites, or is the design of the Russian state no longer to be understood as a genuine federal order? The author argues that the latter is the case.

Andrei Zakharov, who has combined an academic and political career, analyses another consequence of the reforms made in the framework of the establishment of Putin's "power vertical". How has this affected to the role of the Parliament in Russia's young democracy? He paints a rather bleak picture of the way in which the positive progress made in the early years of the newly independent Russia is becoming undone with respect to the development of parliamentarism in today's Russia's.

Overall, the contributors highlight some major achievements in post-Soviet Russia's political system, but also point to some seriously alarming developments indicating that Russia might be diverting from the path towards democracy. It is our modest ambition that the state of affairs offered in this book contributes in one way or another to a further engagement with Russia, in spite of its elusive character.

The Chair InBev-Baillet Latour Spring Lecture Series held at the K.U.Leuven in 2004 and 2005 culminated in this volume.

Leuven, February 2007

AUTHORITY AND IDENTITY IN RUSSIA

Marie Mendras

The question of the state is central in Russia. After the collapse of the Soviet Union in 1991, ruling elites gave more attention to economic restructuring and to power-building than to a profound reform of the state organization. With privatizations and the new market conditions, the state and its organs appeared to be an outmoded system of rule that would impede reforms if given too much weight. Since he became President of Russia, Vladimir Putin has claimed to restore the power and centralizing function of the state. In fact, he is strengthening his office and his own presidential administration at the expense of other public institutions: the government, the Parliament, regional authorities, municipalities, and social institutions like political parties, trade unions, civic associations.

This study seeks first to explain Russian policies with an emphasis on the role of the various public administrations and the lack of a new conception of a democratic state. In a second part, the relations of Russian elites and society toward Europe will be addressed, showing the ambiguity of combined attraction and resistance to Western expectations and norms of conduct.

Authority Building or Power Building?

In the course of 15 years of reforms, from Gorbachev's perestroika to Putin's strategy of central control, state organizations have undergone extensive restructuring. Institutional and financial reforms have reshaped many public bodies. The switch to capitalism has had a powerful impact on modes of governance. Recent developments point to a backlash in state reform, and in the very conception of a federal and democratic system of rule.

The power of administrations

Administrations in Russia have successfully adjusted to the new conditions and have consolidated their positions in the economic, social and political realms. At all territorial levels, they have come out stronger after those years of change and turmoil and more immune to political pressure and legal constraints. This may at first appear to be a surprising phenomenon in a time of state weakness and privatization of the economy. Bureaucracies have demonstrated a remarkable ability to adjust to a changing context and to the emergence of many new actors (private enterprises, financial holdings, foreign investors, citizens, political parties, associations, etc). Our working hypothesis is that, if administrations have reinforced their positions, it means that they have a functionality of their own. They perform tasks that are absolutely crucial to the state and to society at large, and to the individual and to businesses.

Administrations have made themselves indispensable partners of most social actors, from the citizen or public service user to the big oil producer. This is not primarily due to coercion or arbitrary power on their part but, more significantly, on their functionality as organizations and on the diversity amongst administrations, as well as within each administration. The bureaucracy exists as an idea, as a concept, it does not exist as an entity. Codes of conduct in the many state administrations vary greatly. The behaviour of one *chinovnik* may differ widely from that of his colleague next door.

I wish to address the question of the current leadership's attitudes to what is publicly denounced as "over-bureaucratization". Do the leaders show a good understanding of the problem and do they propose convincing responses?

Work in social theory and studies in sociology of organizations have inspired my argument. Herbert Simon, Robert Merton, and Michel Crozier provide rich conceptual frameworks and in-depth analysis of the workings of administrative or entrepreneurial organizations. They oppose the rationalist approach whereby pre-determined conditions and pre-determined goals lead to rational conduct. Crozier and Friedberg recall the 19th century positivist rationalism. Saint Simon, Comte, Hegel, Marx, Lenin predicted the advent of a "rational society". In Saint Simon's words, "the rule of men will be replaced by the administration of things", announcing the end of politics.

The observation of contemporary societies demonstrates that "there are no fully monitored or controlled social systems."[1] "Action and intervention of man on man, i.e. power and its "shameful" side, manipulation and blackmail, are co-substantial to any collective enterprise, precisely because there is no structural and social determinism and because conditioning can never be total".[2] Uncertainty and the indeterminate are key factors in social negotiation, that is to say power politics.

I will argue that at the rhetorical level President Putin tends to adhere to a rationalist vision of his power, whereas in his practical management he

---

[1] Crozier Michel and Friedberg Ehrard, *L'acteur et le système*, Paris: Le Seuil, 1977, p. 29. See also: Crozier Michel, *Le phénomène bureaucratique*. Paris : Le Seuil, 1963.

[2] Ibid., p. 32.

makes ample use of uncertainty and permanent bargaining.

The long historical tradition in administrative clout, under the Tsarist and the Soviet regime, seems to give grounds to the idea that Russia's leaders ruled the empire with a loyal, pyramidal bureaucracy that obeyed orders according to strict hierarchical rules. This was not the case.[3] The sheer size of the country and the harsh climatic conditions gave no other option to central government but to rely heavily on local administrative resources which could not be easily monitored from Moscow or Petersburg.

The very assumption that bureaucracies are, by nature, hierarchical organizations does not hold up to empirical scrutiny. Hierarchy formally exists, but it does not dictate the behaviour of each employee in his daily work. Subordinates do not necessarily inform their superiors. Superiors do not inform their subordinates. Information does not flow easily from one office to the next. Each one sees it as crucial to defend his own margin of autonomy even if he pretends to abide by the formal rules of conduct.

A civil servant enjoys more freedom in his/her work than would appear at first sight. He/she devises his/her own sphere of competence in a way that ensures his/her direct power over a number of decisions and resources. The phenomenon is the same whether the level of decision is low or high on the administrative scale.

The same is true for organizations. A given ministerial or municipal office actually enjoys more autonomy than the formal institutional setup would lead us to believe. An organization builds its power on a certain degree of budgetary self-determination and on the ability to prevent external agents from looking into its domestic politics. To withhold and distort information, to cheat and bluff is one of the keys, in Russia, to achieving a minimal level of discretionary power. And this discretionary power gives the administration the capacity to protect itself from outside interference, to impose its rules on the potential user of the administrative services it provides, and to negotiate with external partners – be they private companies or public bodies.

In keeping with this rationale, Vladimir Putin builds his authority on this natural quest to control information. The President displays his own power if he can control information, play with formal rules and adjust his interpretation of rules he has himself made, as long as he can lie without any great risk of being confronted with it. Paradoxically, his political authority increases with his ability to circumvent the rules, more than with his capacity to build institutional frameworks.

---

[3] Mendras Marie, "Rule by Bureaucracy in Russia", in: Della Porta Donatella and Meny Yves (eds.), *Democracy and Corruption in Europe*, London: Pinter, 1997, pp. 118-131.

The administrative structure of the Russian Federation is not hierarchical. Nor is each administrative structure hierarchical in the way it really functions. Hence, the "power vertical," as Putin likes to define his ideal state pyramid, is not a high-performance centralized machine but the expression of a frustration at not being able to control every actor in Russian political and economic life. Putin's repeated attacks against the federal structure and the spirit of federalism demonstrate his conception of the state: unitary, administrative, resilient to any form of competitive and pluralistic institutional workings.

However, Putin's latest proposals will not build a single transmission belt between the federal level, the regional administrations and the local level of governance. It simply will not work. To explain why Putin's methods are frightening to any supporter of democratic and federal governance but will not effectively work because they are obsolete and unpractical, it is necessary to recall the essential role of bureaucracies in Soviet times.

In Russia after the collapse of the USSR, almost overnight, state administrations took over the strategic functions that the Communist Party structures had performed. It is an interesting feature of post-socialist transformation that an alternative organizational network existed, namely the state structures, which only needed to be activated. The elite in the state structures was not an alternative elite for the simple reason that the men / women were by and large the same, most of them party cadres having direct institutional connections with the party apparatus, and vice versa. Consequently, most administrative bodies retained their specific features, inherited from long years of bureaucratic autonomy-building. Much has been written on clientelism and patrimonial networking in the USSR, and on the general ability of most actors to circumvent strict centralization.[4] Nothing could be less surprising than the sustained differentiation of Russian administrations -in values, in methods, in organizational culture- after the collapse of the one-party system.

Administrations have a functionality and a momentum of their own. They do not remain on the sidelines of major social transformation. They do not fight against it either. They tend to follow in step and guide the movement when possible. They may provide other social actors with some of the instruments to adjust to the new context. One example is the general

---

[4] Solnick Steven, *Stealing the State*, Cambridge, Mass Harvard University Press, 1998; Gill Graeme, "The Soviet Mechanism of Power and the Fall of the Soviet Union", in: Rosenfeld et al. (eds.), *Mechanisms of Power in the Soviet Union*, London and New York: Macmillan, 2002.

social protection that various administrative agencies, especially at the local level, continue to provide to individuals and families. Of course, the given service is not always free and honest but that need not concern us here. Another example is the close interaction between local and regional administrations, and medium and large-size companies. A municipality may not work without a decent budget, and a good part of the budget comes from companies, legally or illegally. Conversely, an enterprise cannot work without the support of administrative organs. Russia remains a country of heavy bureaucratic interference. All operators testify to the long list of pen-pushers they need to court in order to follow through an economic initiative, or simply to obtain an official document.

Administrative arbitrariness of course may impede reform and private initiative. Abusive municipal power in granting or not the right to open a small business or shop can sometimes be qualified as a pure racket.

This nevertheless does not mean that the spontaneous behaviour of civil servants is to resist change. It would be a mistake to view the political leadership in Moscow as essentially reformist and dynamic, and present by contrast state administrations as conservative and nostalgic for the past. Administrations play their part in social change. They do not merely implement policies. They make decisions of their own and demonstrate a good deal of autonomy in their relation with the political leadership, at the federal and provincial level. Administrations have their own dynamics, with their own resources, rooted in clientelism and informal exchanges. They do not confine themselves to implementing decisions taken by others, nor do they keep out of the political scene. In many instances, business and administration have successfully synchronized their mutual interests and have even taken over local politics. Arbakhan Magomedov gives an illustration in the Krasnodar province. The oil business, especially the pipeline project, and administrations have struck a deal which elected politicians could only but accept.[5]

Administrative organs *are* political. The Weberian distinction between the political and the bureaucratic does not hold. Russian politicians, on the Left as well as on the Right, have consistently and loudly attacked the bureaucracies' reactionary attitude and resistance to reform. They have thus promoted the strange idea that politics is dissociated from administration, i.e. daily government of the country. As if political leaders had it all right about reform and bureaucrats all wrong. They claim that political decisions were

---

[5] Magomedov Arbakhan, "Le pétrole de la Caspienne, enjeu politique au Sud de la Russie" in : *La revue Tocqueville/The Tocqueville Review* XXIII, 2002 (no. 2).

apt, implementation failed. The usual rhetoric goes as follows: "Pen-pushers sabotage the major reforms, so cleverly and benevolently designed in the Kremlin. Bureaucrats are allied with the nostalgic Communists and with the backward ordinary Russian in a reactionary attitude." Before Putin came to power, the State Duma as an institution was accused of thwarting progress. Today, the Lower House smoothly follows government prescriptions. And it will hardly be apt to represent the interests of society when the new electoral law comes into force. All deputies will be elected on party lists, and the few parties that will be apt to gather the 7% of votes necessary to get into the Duma, will be working for the Kremlin, or in a "constructive opposition" relationship to the Kremlin (the Communist Party).

Putin's team is playing more and more openly, without any disguise, in a power system devoid of accountability. His 13 September 2004 reforms will make the executive heads of the provinces of the Federation more dependent upon him but less accountable to the people who will no longer elect them.

The immediate gain of such a disconnection between good decisions and failed implementation is the evasion of responsibility. Efficiency is, by essence, measured by users' satisfaction. More often than not, satisfaction is a short-term evaluation of concrete results. Users have trouble assessing the global ability to administer in a long-term perspective. This is even more so in Russia where criticism of public affairs never existed prior to the fall of Communism, and is again severely curtailed today. In European democracies, a long tradition of political participation accounts for strong pressures and potentially unequivocal sanctions on the part of society when it votes out a government. Russian politics today is not truly competitive. Moreover, in Russia, all social actors display a very short time horizon.

It is often said that Russian bureaucracy is excessive. By what criteria can a "reasonable" number of civil servants in a given country be assessed? In fact, Russia has fewer bureaucrats than many European countries. So, from whose point of view are they too many? Society's? Elected officials'? Corporations'? Foreign investors'?

Structurally, any administrative organization has a propensity to grow. It is interesting to observe the self-defensive reflex in expanding size. Indeed, a big organization is more complex, less transparent, less open than a small one. Mass creates protection against outside interference. Very few people in Russia value the advantage of transparent management, in public organizations as well as companies. The tradition of secrecy, distrust for anybody who is not a part of the group and fear of interference favour self-protection over efficiency and competition. The manager sees an interest in keeping information inside the organization, and to do so he needs a complex organization chart that only he can decipher. Redundancy plays a function. It makes it possible to choose between several options and decide who will perform a given duty. Such a strategy gives the necessary leeway to strike deals with private enterprises, to resist central orders, to consolidate local social networks. It also helps diffuse responsibility, a golden rule of conduct in Russia.

As will be discussed below, Putin is using this strategy of building protection around his presidential function by accumulating administrative shields. For bureaucracies should not be seen primarily as obstacles but rather as instruments and protection for the elected officials. The political leadership is to a large extent the hostage of the bureaucratic machine because the machine has rules and habits, it functions as a series of powerful networks with many ties outside state administration, and enjoys a high "paper-legitimacy". It produces official documents that no one can do without, even if one is trying to circumvent the regulation. The main ill of bureaucracy in Russia is not its size, but its complexity, non-transparent networking, and corruption.

Rulers and Ruled

Russia is diverse and unequal. Social differentiation has reached an unprecedented level in an industrialized country at the beginning of the 21st century. Many people live in relatively closed worlds of their own, with little interaction with the outside. To small-town dwellers, Moscow is a distant planet. To Muscovites, provincial life seems remote and unattractive. The countryside remains cut off from much of the process of change.

Yet, in this context of high disparities and semi-autarkic micro-worlds, society exists and is a meaningful subject of study. Russians believe they belong to a national community. It took them time to accept the loss of the Soviet identity and the material security and international image that went with it. They have reframed their loyalties in ways that make them less dependent on federal/national policies. Local affairs, family and work networks are the most pertinent level of an individual's socialization. Non-Russians have a republican-ethnic loyalty, especially in the Volga and North-Caucasus republics. Their common destiny nevertheless is that of the Federation of Russia, with the obvious and dramatic exception of Chechnya, and maybe of other peoples in the Caucasus if Russia continues to wage war.

Today, administrative organization is the essential link that brings together, in one way or other, those various population groups, different territories, and contrasting economic realities. Administrations function as networks, not as rigid hierarchies. They are not cut off from the real world. Depending on their specific competence, they cultivate relations with business, trade unions, foreign partners, politicians, political parties, associations and private citizens. Hence, even if conflicts of interests often oppose them, administration and society at large are not separated.

When Russians complain that the demarcation between the private and the public sphere is blurred, they have in mind that individuals may work in both spheres, and reap benefits from it, and that bureaucracies, like companies, pursue their own corporatist interests rather than those of the ordinary citizen and consumer. But the ordinary citizen, willingly or not, plays in the game of private connections and unwritten rules. If he/she needs a service, he/she spontaneously looks for special access rather than follow the set procedure.

Alena Ledeneva rightly explains that "bribes are not just cases of individual corruption, they are corrections of a malfunctioning system of prices for public services". Hence, "people behave strategically."[6] The definition of corruption is not universal. In Russia, bribes are often viewed as natural elements of exchange.

People know they have a better chance of finding a solution in a municipal office or ministry department because, there, employees have more negotiating resources at their disposal. This explains why many disputes tend to be resolved inside administrations instead of in court. Why turn to justice if court decisions are slow, often partial, and rarely enforced?[7] Russians are critical of their bureaucracies but they rely on them for lack of a better alternative. They do not trust them in principle but they come to trustworthy agreements with state sector employees. As to judicial power, they do not trust it and do not turn to it if they can avoid it. Another consequence of Putin's reform of September 2004 is the increased control from the President over the nomination and dismissal of judges.

In Russia, neither Gorbachev nor Yeltsin found themselves under strong pressure from society to democratize. If such pressures came from the Baltic societies, and to some extent from Armenia, Georgia, western Ukraine, conveyed by the national elites of those republics, the same cannot be said of the Russian republic's population. Russians did not fight for civil liberties and democracy. It does not mean that many of them did not long for them, but they welcomed the radical change of political values as a

---

[6] Ledeneva Alena, *Non-transparency of the post-Communist economies*, paper presented at the Honesty and Trust Workshop, Budapest, November 2002.

[7] Holmes Stephen (ed.), "Reforming Russia's Courts" in: *East European Constitutional Review*, 2002, 11/1-2.

necessary path to get out of the severe economic and cultural depression of the 1980s. Western-style democracy did not form a neatly packed set of values that Russians had cultivated for years. It was an immediate solution, an alternative model to replace the old, and it was more reassuring than facing the vacuum left by the sudden disintegration of the Soviet system.

In a previous work[8] I argue that the building of a democratic regime is not the Russians' priority. My point is not that they are undemocratic, or oblivious to fundamental values such as honesty and individual freedom. To them, by force of circumstance, democratization was a "no-choice" alternative. Soviet Communism having been disqualified, the only familiar course was a western-style market economy and democracy, hopefully conducive to prosperity. In the Soviet mentality, dichotomy had reigned. Everything was explained in black and white, either-or formulas. This legacy hinders a more critical understanding of social change and the meaning of democracy. For instance, the "rule of law" which was a very popular slogan in the late Gorbachev years, probably had a restricted meaning among the Soviet population. It was understood in terms of social justice and some form of leadership accountability, not much beyond that.

What many Russians most resent about the transition is firstly material insecurity, frustration at not having gained much, or having lost a lot, since 1991 when the happy few seized the national wealth, and secondly the clear revelation of what they could not quite express before: the low image they have of themselves.

Insecurity and unpredictability are new anxieties. Under the Soviet regime, exchanges followed a particular pattern. Time was not as short as it is today. Negotiations, at a private or public level, could take for ever. Years ahead looked the same, prices were fixed, no interest rates, not much money to earn, no real estate frenzy... The system worked on a permanent exchange of donations and counter-donations. The specificity of the immobile, non monetary and closed Soviet world, was that time extended far ahead. You could get some desired scarce good or service and "pay it back" years later. And vice versa, you might have to deliver some good or service immediately knowing you will reap the benefit much later. Today, time is extremely short because the horizon lacks security or predictability.

Secondly, Russians have a low image of themselves. What is left of their past after the devastating official denunciation of the Soviet failure? What positive references have replaced the old doctrine and the old values? If they

---

[8] Mendras Marie, « La préférence pour le flou. Pourquoi la construction d'un régime démocratique n'est pas la priorité des Russes » in : *Le Débat*, 1999 (November-December), no 107, pp. 35-50.

compare themselves to the western model of political, social and economic achievement, they see how far they are from it, and this is very discouraging. Westernization in the sense of striving to meet western standards of social conduct and economic prosperity no longer looks attainable nor desirable.

In my paradigm of preference for the indeterminate, I also argue that the rulers and the ruled equally share this preference. It is as gross a mistake to oppose a "democratic, reform-oriented" political elite to a backward and reactionary man-in-the-street, as it is to oppose a cynical, dishonest, potentially authoritarian leadership to a liberal-minded society deprived of democracy and "westernization". Russian elites are not at loggerheads with society.

There is a striking discrepancy between Putin's favorable rating and the great distrust of state institutions in society. Maybe an explanation can be found in the symbolic nature of the President as a national figure. Putin is popular for what he stands for: his resolution to avoid chaos, to stabilize the situation, to sustain very cautious reforms, even if he claims a more reformist streak in his speeches. And he helps rehabilitate Russia's image abroad. Putin does not seem to be rated for what he promises to do or for his style of government. He is valued for the function he represents, more than for his personality or strategies. By contrast, his presidential administration and his government have not won the trust of the population. And we see few signs that trust might increase. Interestingly, the Church and the army draw more positive attitudes than other social institutions. This may also be explained by the fact that those two institutions carry an important symbolic function, like the Presidency. But they do not govern. Opinion surveys reveal profound distrust toward every institution that is directly involved in daily management, at the local, regional and national level.

Putin, champion of the state or agent of its demise?

Putin is claiming to be strengthening the state, but actually he is undermining the very fundaments of the federal and democratic institutions of state rule.

He seems to be pursuing a strategy of "rule by decree", together with pushing legislation through the Duma. But at the same time he criticizes the "over-extended bureaucracy" and announces that the number of civil servants must be curbed. This raises a contradiction. If the government wants to implement structural reforms, it needs to make demands on state organs. He cannot load the administrative system with new tasks and tell them they are inefficient and too costly.

President Putin gives the impression of addressing an acute crisis of governance with obsolete instruments. He talks of restoring the "state pyramid" or "power vertical" when it is clear that re-centralization and primitive control over institutions, state officials and enterprises will not work.

Russian officials display a disconcerting propensity to present the situation in their country as utterly dismal and to advance the miraculous formula that will make it converge with the more experienced western democracies.

In his attack against "over-bureaucratization", Putin caught himself in a full-blown contradiction. He claims to engage in significant administrative restructuring and he legitimizes the reforms with an ideology of progress and efficiency, and a resolute attack against corruption. But he is actually creating more bureaucracy and making political functions, in the government and in regional executive organs, more bureaucratic, les accountable, no longer elected, and directly related to a very heavy and closed administrative structure, the presidential administration. The latest reforms of September 2004 are an indirect acknowledgment of the utter failure of the state reform so far.

The anti-corruption drive offers another example of ill-suited policies. Extensive literature exists on the difficulty to combat corruption and administrative abuse of power.[9] As Shelley notes, "President Putin does not understand that a sustained and successful campaign against these phenomena, as has occurred in Italy, requires the partnership of civil society and the media."[10] Klyamkin believes that the only fragile motivation in combating illegality and corruption might come from businessmen, especially in small business.[11] Is the absence of strong political will the severest impediment to anti-corruption policies? I remain cautious as to the capacity of the Russian government, even if it really wanted to curb corruption, to do so effectively.

Tompson quotes an instance where bureaucratic inefficiency was not the primary cause of a social crisis: "As Putin acknowledged in early 2001, the energy shortages that hit much of Siberia and the Far East during the coldest months of winter were not only the product of administrative incompetence

---

[9] See Klyamkin Igor, *Burokratiya i biznes*, paper presented at the Centre d'études et de recherches internationales, Sciences-Po, Paris, 15 November 2002; Shelley Louise, "Can Russia Fight Organized Crime and Corruption?" in: *La revue Tocqueville/The Tocqueville Review* XXIII, 2002 (no.2); among many others.

[10] Shelley Louise, "Can Russia Fight Organized Crime and Corruption?" in: *La revue Tocqueville/The Tocqueville Review* XXIII, 2002 (no.2)

[11] Klyamkin Igor, *Burokratiya i biznes*, paper presented at the Centre d'études et de recherches internationales, Sciences-Po, Paris, 15 November 2002.

and corruption, important though these factors were. They also reflected the inefficiency of the largely unreformed utilities sector and the decay of an infrastructure that cannot be renewed in the absence of a fundamental reform of the system of housing and municipal subsidies."[12]

Putin finds himself conducting an ambivalent policy: he is trying to restore the strength of the state by raising its coerciveness, or capacity to resort to coercion. The disastrous war in Chechnya and the increased pressure on the media are cases in point. In doing so, democratic government and civil liberties are receding. Citizens and economic operators will turn even more to administrations for stability and predictability. Bureaucratic modes of management will not abate. If Putin had chosen honest competition, free information and political transparency, and full support for the building of an independent judicial system, maybe administrations would have to behave more openly and more respectfully of society's interests.

Identity: European or Not?

The focus of my analysis here is Russian perceptions and attitudes toward the European sphere. How do the elites and the Russian public view Europe and our modes of living and governing? And on the basis of this knowledge, how can we adjust and devise profitable policies toward Russia?

My main arguments will be organized as follows. Firstly, Europe is not the West but a well-defined and specific part of the western world, the two notions are clearly separated in Russians' minds. Secondly, the ruling elites and society are not at odds on the issue of neighbouring Europe. For all, Europe is a highly attractive region in terms of way of life, but effective rapprochement with the European Union and its demanding rules of conduct seems to be an unattainable goal. Thirdly, European countries, and EU institutions, could build more effectively on the favourable dispositions of Russians to strive to install more solid bases for good neighbourly relations, and should not hesitate to exert some pressure on the Russian government when need be, most notably in issues of Human Rights and civil liberties and in pushing for a solution to end the devastating war in Chechnya.

Russia and the West

For decades, the notion of "zapad", the West, was prominent in official Soviet discourse. The doctrinal line read that the United States fully controlled its allies and that western European allies had little say in NATO affairs and

---

[12] Tompson William, "Putin's Challenge: The Politics of Structural Reform in Russia" in: *Europe-Asia Studies*, 2002, Vol. 54, no 6, pp.933-957.

more generally in strategic affairs. What was said of military supremacy was also said of economics, namely that America and the dollar were guiding the capitalist world. There was very little in Soviet rhetoric, not surprisingly, about the diversity of political regimes and cultures. Hence, no serious reflection was ever conducted publicly on western types of democratic regimes and social systems. In the Soviet Union, the values of democracy remained hostage to the East-West divide, a black-and-white dichotomy between the so-called "socialist democracy" and the usurped "capitalist democracy".

Paradoxically, the western world was at the very centre of the Soviet system. The West was Russia's alter ego. The myth of a hostile and unjust Western civilization legitimized the Soviet Union. Economic and political arbitrariness were justified in terms of confrontation with the USA. The population had to accept sacrifices imposed by what was a virtual state of war. The West was not only a convenient scapegoat but also a standard, even a model. The USSR had to do better than the capitalists, to surpass their economies. Competition was the very essence of the Soviet system. In negating Western civilization the Soviet leadership had to refer to it constantly.

Western European political culture had not been totally eradicated in the elite's consciousness. It was the only well-known alternative, and Europe was geographically and culturally close. In the last years of Gorbachev, Western democracies were clearly taken as a model, or goal. In the years 1991-92, everybody spoke of a transition to the Western system. What was most attractive to the Soviet population was the better living standards of average Europeans and Americans compared to the average Russian: more comfort, more choice, more fun, and some form of social protection, especially in European countries. For a majority of Russians in the early 1990s, an improvement in material conditions prevailed over other aims. Institutional reforms, human rights or a free press were not as valued as a rise in living standards. Maybe one reason for this attitude is that basic rights and freedoms had already been granted by Gorbachev's regime in the late 1980s. Free voting, political parties, independent media, open borders were all achievements -even if not fully consolidated- of the *perestroika* and *glasnost* years. And they had been won peacefully, without struggle or social rebellion (with the exception of the Baltic states and the Caucasus). Russians did not fight for liberties and freedoms, which may explain why they see them as granted, although for generations they had been deprived of the most basic rights.

In spite of propaganda, Soviet people intuitively knew that one lived better on the other side of the Wall. They also believed that American capitalism was the wicked system imposed on European societies that would otherwise lean toward greater equality and more socialist policies. To the educated Soviet public in the 1970s and 1980s, Sweden no doubt came out as the successful model of combined socialism and capitalism. And France was traditionally perceived as the nicest country with *art de vivre* and culture. Evil in the West was epitomised by the US, the Pentagon and the arrogant billionaire. Responsibility lay with Washington more than with western European capitals. Hence, no deep hostility accumulated against Europe. It is important to recall the mentality inherited from the Soviet period to understand the reasons behind Russian attitudes. In the event of crisis, the fundamental hostility toward America quickly re-emerges and the Putin-controlled media can easily manufacture dreadful accounts of the White House's scenarios of conquest and domination. Similarly, French or German opposition to US policies are over-interpreted as the rebellion of the younger brothers in the wake of the Cold War dynamics.

Two remarkable examples are the NATO strikes against Serbia in 1999 and the war in Iraq. In the spring of 1999, the Russian authorities and the media waged a very hostile campaign against the Kosovo war, openly defending the Serbian government and heralding the principle of non interference in a sovereign state's domestic affairs. NATO strikes were presented on Russian television as US strikes. The public quickly adhered to the anti-American rhetoric, and hostility towards America was higher than ever in opinion polls. As soon as the war ended and the media turned to other subjects, hostility ebbed away and came back not to its pre-Kosovo level but to a moderate distrust toward America.

The Russian public reacted with horror and sympathy towards Americans after the dramatic September 2001 attacks in New York. It shows that they no longer are in a demonised Cold War vision of the US. But when the war in Iraq started, once again without UN approval, the same scenario unfolded. Media barked against Washington, and anti-American feelings again exacerbated. In contrast, West European criticism of US methods, Great Britain excepted, reinforced the sense of proximity with Europe.

The irony is that President Putin carefully maintained a close relationship with President Bush before, during and after the military campaign in Iraq and that he comfortably combined a pragmatic strategy toward Washington and an orchestrated opposition to US international policies at home. Consequently, his ostentatious collaboration with the French President and the German Chancellor in opposing US "unilateralism" during the very tense first months of 2003 amounted more to a clever dual policy than to any meaningful "alliance" with Paris and Berlin.

Whatever the international context, the US remains the Russian state's number 1 strategic partner. The European Union is not seen in Moscow as a serious strategic actor. Russian authorities traditionally prefer bilateral relations to multilateral policies. This is obvious in its dealings with the EU and with NATO. With the "socialist" Eastern part of Europe, they never really had to monitor relationship of equals within an alliance. The Warsaw Pact was not a free will alliance but imposed upon Central European states. Today, Russia has no close ally and belongs to no alliance, considering that the Commonwealth of Independent States (CIS) does not provide the foundations for any serious multilateral economic or military system.

This lack of experience, added to the trauma of having lost both the Eastern European satellites and the Soviet republics, explains why the Yeltsin government found itself incapable of devising new relations or new policies with the former forced "allies" and colonised territories of the former Russian empire. In the 1990s, Russia was watching, powerless, the rapid westernisation and Europeanisation of Eastern Europe and the Baltic states, and the tentative rapprochement of Ukraine to Europe.

In the last two years, the Russian and the Ukrainian Presidents have made much effort in the direction of a political and economic rapprochement. Kuchma's weakness at home, on the eve of the Ukrainian presidential election in the autumn of 2004, led him to accept Putin's propositions. They met in Yalta in July 2004 and Kuchma gave in, at least on the surface, and said that Ukraine no longer sees membership of the European Union as a priority.

Europe, the Preferred Other

For most Russians, the European Union is a success: peace, prosperity along with social justice, and traditional culture are better protected there than anywhere else. These three values are held high in Russia.

Western European states have successfully eradicated war among themselves and put an end to the disastrous colonial conflicts. To the Russians, who have lived for decades in a "war scare" environment, this is an extraordinary accomplishment. Under the Soviet regime, the idea that a major war might be launched at any minute weighed heavily on people's minds. And the inevitability of conflict and violence continues to pervade. Putin's administration unscrupulously uses this inherited vulnerability to instill doubt and insecurity in society. Consequently, people are more submissive and more prone to accept arbitrary policies. For example, with the probability of terrorist acts still high, the state can advocate violent responses and justify them in the eyes of the public. The disastrous war in Chechnya fits the picture.

In this respect, the U.S.'s unilateral decision to resort to military means in Iraq had a dramatic impact on Russian perceptions and on elites' self-justification. If democratic and powerful America can do it, then why criticise Russia for "combating terror" in Chechnya by waging war? If America can disregard the law in dealing with the Afghan war and Iraqi detainees, why should Moscow worry about violation of human rights and excessive violence in the north Caucasus? Even though a few European countries have joined the military campaign in Iraq, Russians see it as a US war, and do not associate Europe with it. Hence, the gap between a peaceful and peace-keeping Europe and a warmongering America is widening.

Prosperity along with social justice is the second major achievement of European societies. Russians are convinced that America's wealth is much less equitably distributed across society. Better living standards are precisely what Russians expect from Putin's rule. As Yuri Levada's polls show, they are satisfied with the relative improvement in daily matters, such as timely wage payments, but concerned about the fragility of their situation and the probability that things will not continue to improve in the near future. When the Russian official media speak proudly of the new "stability", one should be aware that it is not perceived in society as a long-term stabilisation.

The third attraction is Europe's traditional culture. Most educated Russians have some notions about French literature, German music and Italian art. They know very little about North American history and culture. This faithful tribute to European heritage may be on the wane. The younger generation is less educated in the humanities and the arts and more attracted to American law and economics. To an average Russian, America remains a very remote and unknown universe whereas Europe is closer and, even if not accessible to him / her, more friendly in his / her imagination.

Disenchantment

The dark side of the medal is growing resentment against the complex and strict rules of European Union policies. In the months before the May 1st 2004 entry of ten new members, the Russian government grew nervous and erratic in its renegotiation of its partnership with the EU. The balance of power was not favourable to Russia, which eagerly sought to reach agreements before the candidate states became effectively members of the European Union. As former socialist countries they were prone to behave more harshly towards Moscow. One of the constant pressures exerted by

Moscow on the EU has been the "unequal treatment" of Russian-speaking populations in Latvia and Estonia.

The real issue in relations between Russians and us, Europeans, and Westerners more generally, is the problem of influence. It has grown increasingly unpleasant for Russian elites to find themselves under the powerful influence of their wealthier neighbours. They fear they are losing their independence and becoming obedient followers of western patrons. They resent the fact that international organisations and international norms are essentially pro-western. And they tend to refuse the constraint of western-style modernisation and democratisation. The fact that no serious alternative to western European modernisation exists makes Russian elites feel that we are imposing our model on them.

Western politicians, consultants and experts certainly share considerable responsibility for this misunderstanding with Russians about the fast transition to a market economy and a liberal democracy. Most were short-sighted and romantic about the prospects of a smooth Russian transition comparable to that of the Central European states. They did not pay sufficient attention to the social and cultural situation in post-Soviet Russia and to the heavy legacy of entrenched bad habits: clientelism, paternalism, corruption, dismissal of responsibility, lack of accountability. One of the most troubling features of Putin's Russia is the confusion between the private and the public spheres and the benefits that many, in both the state apparatus and in big business, reap from this welcome confusion.

Russians suffer from unfulfilled expectations from Europe. They nevertheless continue to value Europe as the closest and safest partner. In a series of surveys conducted by the Foundation for Public Opinion in 2001, 2002 and 2003, attraction to Europe is clearly on the rise: 73% believe that Russia should seek membership in the European Union, 10% think it should not and 18% find it hard to answer. In 2001, the respective percentages were 59% for, 19% against and 22 who give no answer. (FOM opinion polls, site English.fom.ru) Not surprisingly, the young and the educated are more likely to desire joining the EU. There are regional differences too. In the Far East, interest is much less marked than in southern and western regions.

The idea is to profit from the proximity with Europe, from the money poured into cooperation and from cultural exchanges, but Russians repeat that they are distinct. They do not say they fully belong to Europe except when they adopt the rhetorical figure of "We, Europeans" versus either China or the US. As the geographer Vladimir Kolossov explains, "Russia is a Eurasian country by its geographic situation but in cultural terms and in self-identification, it claims to be European. However, other aspects of

Russian culture, in particular the relation between rulers and ruled is far from being European."[13] If you state as a premise and a promise that you will be like Europe, you know it will be so hard economically and politically that you will always lag behind, and this is very uncomfortable and unpleasant after decades or Communist rule with the dismal result of having always lagged behind the US.

Russian Domestic Affairs Matter

Vladimir Putin's greatest achievement has been to dissociate his domestic policies from foreign policy matters. By and large, Western governments have tacitly agreed to turn a blind eye on Russia's growing disregard for democratic rule and human rights. They do not wish such unpleasant considerations to stand in the way of strategic and political relations with the Kremlin. Most European heads of state and government prefer to praise the Russian President's "public engagement in favour of reforms" and his claim to be a "modern leader". The official rhetoric is so easily accepted. On important matters of state behaviour, only governments and international institutions, with their authority and potential for influence, can confront the Russian leadership over misguided policies that violate basic principles and jeopardise security. This was not done in the case of Chechnya. The west did not interfere nor even try to influence the Kremlin. The war in Chechnya is Yeltsin's and Putin's greatest shame and the international community's greatest failure in its treatment of post-Soviet Russia.

Foreign states and international institutions are presently confronted with a very confusing and unpredictable Russian polity. Since the fall of the Soviet Union, political dialogue between western governments and the Russian state has remained very traditional and has progressively lost much of its intensity and significance. Summit meetings and intergovernmental committees are strikingly disconnected from the other domains of interaction.

As a long-time student of Russia and a social scientist, I find it impossible to dissociate foreign policy from domestic developments. One cannot evade the question of the regime drift away from pluralism, political competition and the protection of civil liberties. The war in Chechnya, the Yukos case, the dependence of the judiciary, the control of the media, uncompetitive elections all testify to the decline in democratic values and behaviour. Putin's discourse at home is more and more critical of foreign influence.

---

[13] Kolossov Vladimir, *Mir glazami rossii: mify i vneshnaya politika (The world in the eyes of Russians: myths and Foreign Policy)*, Moscow, Institute of the Foundation of Public Opinion (FOM), 2003.

His attack on NGOs in his address to the Duma in June 2004, the noisy propaganda about Russian speakers in the Baltic states, his pressures on the Ukrainian government to move closer to Russia and away from Europe all illustrate this. The public speech varies according to the audience. At home, it looks productive to be hard on the West and on some aspects of European policies. Abroad, in talks with his counterparts, Putin is "modern", pro-western, and complains about the pressures from his society that is supposedly less progressive and more keen to save Russia's "specificity". We saw above that this does not honestly reflect the Russian society's attitudes.

The fundamental question today is whether the shrinking of the public debate in Russia, the control of the media and the fight against high profile members of the political and economic elites, which is the general trend of the regime, will slowly erode the special relationship and the projects of partnership with Europe.

Distinctness and proximity with Europe, self-accomplishment and recognition from Europe are the ideals of a very large segment of Russians. The diffuse but ongoing influence of the West, especially Europe, remains very strong. There still is in Russia a " European exception ", by which I mean a special relation to the European cultural and social heritage. The relationship of Russia to Europe has been, is, and will be important, yet ambivalent, in the future. Europe is the key to Russia's integration into the international system, no longer as a superpower but as an average modern state.

RUSSIAN NATIONALISM UNDER PUTIN: A MAJORITY FAITH?

Luke March

Judging by much coverage, Russian nationalism is *the* story of contemporary Russian politics. Indeed, a "humiliated" former superpower beset by rampaging crime and appalling socio-economic problems has seemed at times a prime candidate for succumbing either to Yugoslav-style ethnic conflict or a "Weimar" scenario with revanchist forces threatening to win via the ballot box.[1] Latterly Putin's regime has demonstrated ostensibly "nationalistic" features both domestically and internationally, with its ham-fisted involvement in the Ukrainian "Orange Revolution" one of the most obvious examples.

Yet despite assertive nationalistic rhetoric at times appearing the *lingua franca* of Russian domestic and foreign policy, it is precisely the absence of mass ethnic mobilization, electoral success for ethno-political parties (after the decline of the red-brown opposition" in the mid-1990s), widespread ethnic unrest and revanchist foreign policy throughout the 1990s that is most striking on closer view. Explaining this apparent paradox is at the centre of analysis here. We focus on several key factors: Russia's imperial history, which hampered the emergence of both civic and ethnic nationalisms; weak mass-elite linkages that have prevented the mobilization of ethno-nationalist ideas; effective management of nationalist sentiments by the political elite, and a relatively benign international environment. Russian nationalism is by no means the majority faith of ethnic Russians today, but there are indications under Putin that it remains a potent potential issue, and may be increasing in significance again.

Strong Empire, Weak Nation

The emergence of a distinct Russian people can be traced to the tenth century A.D., when eastern Slavic peoples occupying present day Belarus, Ukraine and European Russia were consolidated by Kievan princes into a linguistic and cultural community possessing a relatively high level of

---

[1] A full treatment of the "Weimar Russia" thesis is Aleksandr Yanov, *Posle El'tsina: "Veimarskaya" Rossiya*, Moscow: KRUK, 1995. The thesis is critiqued in Hanson Stephen E. and Kopstein Jeffrey S., "The Weimar/Russia Comparison" in: *Post-Soviet Affairs*, 1997, 13/3, pp. 252-283.

agricultural, commercial and technological development. In 988 Prince Vladimir I of Kievan Rus' brought Byzantine Orthodox Christianity to Kiev. The subsequent religious conversion of the peoples of Rus' gradually produced a distinct political and cultural system, which had developed its own customary legal code, the *Pravda Russkaya* (Russian Law), by the Eleventh century.[2]

Situated on a vast plain, the east Slavic tribes were exposed from the outset to the cultural influences and military pretensions of neighbouring peoples. The Golden Horde's conquest of Kievan Rus' in 1240 had long-lasting effects, dividing Russians from Europe and from Belorussians and Ukrainians, who thereafter came under Polish and Lithuanian influence. When an independent Muscovy emerged from the decaying Khanate at the end of the fifteenth century, its leaders sought to rebuild the nascent cultural-linguistic community by focussing on state-building and defense. The Orthodox Church, the cradle of east Slavic community throughout Mongol tutelage, propagated Russia's mission as the "Third Rome", and was used by the state to attract the loyalty of scattered peoples.[3]

According to the historian Vasilii Klyuchevskii, "colonization in a boundless plain is the fundamental fact of Russian history".[4] "Gathering the lands" resulted in continuous Russian territorial expansion into contiguous territories until the twentieth century. As expansion occurred simultaneously with internal political consolidation, Russia was from the outset a multinational empire, and unlike many maritime empires evolved no distinction between core imperial nation and peripheral colonies.[5] This peculiarity led to several unique features. While *prima facie* the Russian empire privileged ethnic Russian culture and religion with a national ideology entailing universal claims, the building of a powerful imperial state continually impeded the political-cultural self-definition of the numerically dominant Russians by subordinating it to the needs of a repressive and absolutist imperialist monarchy.[6]

---

[2] Unless otherwise noted, this historical overview is derived from Hosking Geoffrey, *Russia and the Russians,* London: Penguin, 2001, and Hosking Geoffrey, *Russia: People and Empire 1552-1917,* London: HarperCollins, 1997.

[3] For a full treatment, see Duncan Peter, *Russian Messianism: Third Rome, Revolution, Communism and After,* London: Routledge, 2000.

[4] Klyuchevskii V. O., *Sochineniya,* Moscow: Gozpolitizdat, 1956, vol. 1, p. 32.

[5] Theen Rolf H. W., "Quo vadis, Russia? The problem of National Identity and State Building" in: Smith Gordon B. (ed.), *State Building in Russia: The Yeltsin Legacy and the Challenge of the Future,* Armonk, New York: M. E. Sharpe, 1999.

[6] Theen, "Quo vadis, Russia?"; Rowley David G., "Imperial Versus National Discourse: the Case of Russia" in: *Nations and Nationalism,* 2000, 6/1, pp. 23-42.

Indeed, nationalism as such, with aspirations to a supra-local collective community sharing common myths, culture and political rights, is alien to the Russian tradition. By the sixteenth century one can certainly identify a clear Russian *ethnie*, Anthony Smith's concept of a proto-nation sharing symbols, history, culture and territory but not yet aspirations to political self-determination.[7] Indeed, Russian "nationalism" was always state-led and directed, not popularly mobilized. Until the 1830s the Tsarist Empire promoted a supranational Russian imperial identity (*Rossiiskii* in Russian), implying a non-ethnic territorial-civic identity ("all those who live in Russia") as opposed to *Russkii* (denoting "ethnic Russians"). Imperial subjects' loyalty was supposed to be to land, faith, state and Tsar, above all to the latter, who remained until 1917 the representative of God on Earth. Identity was tied to imperial institutions rather than the people themselves and to this date the word nation (*natsiya*) has far less currency in Russian than words like state (*gosudarstvo*) or people (*narod*). As Anatol Lieven notes, for centuries Russian national identity has been focussed on non-ethnic allegiances: "imperial, religious and ideological".[8] The central identity of the "Russian" empire was "Orthodox", not "Russian".[9]

However, by the nineteenth century Russia was beginning to develop some of the features of modernity that scholars such as Ernest Gellner believe to be necessary for the emergence of nationalism proper. These included increasingly vibrant commercial sectors, an ever more educated and literate population, gradual political liberalization and the penetration of Western political thought. Indeed, contact with Europe provoked national feelings in the form of *ressentiment* – the reaction against a perceived dominant and superior neighbouring culture. In the debate between so-called "Westerners" and "Slavophiles" from the 1830s onwards the intelligentsia grappled with Russia's ostensible backwardness, the latter group (conservative thinkers such as Ivan Kireevskii and Aleksei Khomyakov) took the view that Russia should pursue its own distinctive cultural course and cultivate its Orthodox traditions in order to avoid the afflictions of Western capitalism and culture.

From the 1830s the Russian state moved increasingly towards Russification. Reflecting this trend were the ideas of the Pan-Slavists (such as Nikolai Danilevskii and Fedor Dostoevskii) who argued for imperial expansion into Europe in defence of Slavic culture. Yet "Russification" was still a limited

---

[7] Smith Anthony D., *The Ethnic origins of Nations*, Oxford: Blackwell, 1986, p. 163.
[8] Lieven Anatol, "The weakness of Russian nationalism" in: *Survival*, 1999, 41/2, pp. 53-70 at p. 55.
[9] Ibid., p. 63.

state-sponsored "official" nationality. This was famously demonstrated in 1833 by Nicholas I's minister Count Uvarov, who argued for public education in the spirit of "Orthodoxy, Autocracy, and Nationality". The last was undoubtedly the least important — tellingly, the Russian *narodnost'* really means "closeness to the people", and is a relationship of state to subjects, rather than a call to popular ethnic sentiment. Indeed, the Tsars saw even the Pan-Slavists as heretical, for implying that the state served ethnic Russian interests rather than *vice versa*.[10] With Russians making up only 43.3 per cent of the population of the empire in 1897, pandering to their whims threatened serious instability.

Moreover, the chasm separating elite and people in Tsarist Russia, a rigidly hierarchical society with few institutionalized links between state and local communities, drastically impeded the emergence of a coherent or mass-based Russian nationalist movement. While the creation of an ethnic Russian identity was thwarted, the civic identity implicit in the *Rossiiskoe* state was weakened by the absence of civic institutions demanding widespread loyalty. Russian modernization was sporadic, and largely confined to urban pockets such as St Petersburg and Moscow. Russia as a whole remained a predominately agricultural country, poorly linked by communications or embedded civil institutions such as political parties. Even deep into the Soviet period, local identity was more important than national identity, particularly for the numerically dominant peasantry. So the Tsarist state, through lack of will and ability, ultimately failed to construct a coherent popular Russian nationalism to replace the imperial identity, which was eventually critically weakened by military defeat (in 1905 and 1914-17) and Tsarist misrule. Until the end of Tsarism, state-sponsored nationalism was largely reactive, a response to the rise of nationalism in Europe and an attempt to stave off the coming revolution. Increasing desperation was shown by the overt anti-Semitism allowed by the government in 1903-6. Geoffrey Hosking describes this as a "poor man's patriotism" – employed in order to mobilize support for a regime from which many were increasingly alienated.[11]

Russian nationalism emerged no stronger from Soviet rule, not least because of the USSR's adherence to a supranational ideology (Marxism-Leninism) that denied nationalism a discourse. Nevertheless, once the envisaged global proletarian revolution had failed to materialize, Stalin's attempt to create "socialism in one country" from the mid-1920s onwards was implicitly proto-nationalistic, stressing defence of the international revolution in its Soviet homeland. Indeed, many see the Great Patriotic (in

---

[10] Rowley, "Imperial versus national discourse", p. 26.
[11] Hosking, *Russia and the Russians*, p. 344.

Russian *otechestvennyi* — "Fatherland") War of 1941-45 as the culmination of the transformation of Soviet patriotism into a Russian nationalism, when Soviet regime and Russian people were as one. Some Russian nationalists even go as far as to see Stalin as "the greatest anti-communist of the twentieth century".[12] After all, Stalin presided over the resurrection of the role of the Orthodox church, imperial Russian historical and literary figures, and Russification policies aimed at the USSR's fourteen non-Russian national republics, while Marxism-Leninism was downplayed in Stalinist wartime ideology.

Although state and people were united by the war as never before, Soviet and Tsarist attitudes towards Russian nationalism were remarkably similar. The Soviets tolerated more statist/imperial "national Bolshevism" in order better to inject an emotional, patriotic and spiritual content into Soviet discourse in the service of the state, especially in the Brezhnev period (1964-1982). National Bolshevism was an ideology originating in émigré circles in the 1920s that justified Soviet power from a national-imperial not Marxist-Leninist point-of-view, i.e. because it strengthened Russian superpower status and not because it was (supposedly) building a classless society.[13] Yet the Soviet regime was essentially "vampirical" upon Russian nationalism.[14] It manipulated only those manifestations that were supportive of Soviet rule, draining them of autonomy and suppressing any overt threats to the USSR's delicate ethnic balance. Russian identity was relatively successfully alloyed with Soviet identity, yet while other republics increasingly identified Russians as the imperial nation, the Russian Soviet Republic (RSFSR) was denied many quasi-state institutions given to the other republics (such as a capital, ministries and republican Party organization). Russian cultural traditions, such as Orthodoxy, remained under constant threat of repression.

The unresolved status of Russians within the Soviet Union was one of the major factors contributing to its collapse. Latent ethnic Russian discontent with their status as colonized colonizers emerged belatedly in response to demands for secession and sovereignty in the other Union republics. However, the nationalist reaction did not quickly unseat Soviet power, as in many other republics. Indeed, nationalists split into two camps: "empire savers", who identified the nation with the Soviet state, and "nation-builders" who saw Soviet power as detrimental to the Russian nation.[15] Although

---

[12] *Den'*, 15-21 August 1993.
[13] A detailed treatment of national Bolshevism is given by Agursky Mikhail, *The Third Rome: National Bolshevism in the USSR*, Boulder: Westview, 1987.
[14] Lieven, "The weakness of Russian nationalism", p. 64.
[15] See Dunlop John B., *The Rise of Russia and the Fall of the Soviet Empire*, Princeton: Princeton University Press, 1993.

many "empire-saving" Russian nationalists allied with Soviet conservatives to defend the Soviet state, they remained hampered both by their alliance with the increasingly unpopular communists and unwillingness to mobilize in the electoral arena until far later than their democratic opponents. In contrast, Boris Yeltsin's election as Russian president in June 1991 on a "nation-saving" platform of Russian autonomy and democracy apparently marked the first occurrence of a Russian "civic" nationalism potentially unencumbered by the burdens of empire.[16]

Nevertheless, the potential for Russian civic nationalism remained just that. The preservation of Russian autonomy within a looser union was the anticipated goal of most "nation-savers", Yeltsin included. Yet with the demise of the USSR in December 1991 Russia, with no history as a nation-state independent of empire, had lost territory it had occupied for over three centuries, including the historic heartlands of Kievan Rus'. When rapid global and domestic decline were added to the volatile mix of insecure and immature borders and imperial nostalgia it is unsurprising that the nation-building coalition soon fragmented. Russians now made up 82 per cent of the population of the new (still multinational) state, as opposed to 51 per cent of the population of the USSR in 1991. On one hand, the prospects of forming a coherent nation-state were arguably far better than ever. From another perspective, this greatly increased the danger of aggressive Russian nationalism, with there being no other ethnic groups within the Russian state that could act as an effective counterweight.

Contemporary Russian Ethnopolitics

"The Russian question" – the relationship between a putative Russian "nation-state" and its former empire, and between the Russian majority and the numerous minorities in the Russian multinational state – has been so important in post-Soviet Russia that almost all political groups have engaged with it. However the sheer number of such groups is no indication of their influence. On the contrary, it emphasizes deep divisions over the national idea and the weakness of institutionalized group politics occasioned by Russia's rapid exposure to full political pluralism.

Five key approaches to the Russian question can be identified, which are by no means mutually exclusive:[17]

---

[16] Breslauer G. W. and Dale C., "Boris Yeltsin and the Invention of a Russian Nation-State" in: *Post-Soviet Affairs*, 1997, 33/3, pp. 303-332.

[17] These categories are based on Tolz Vera, "Values and the Construction of a National Identity" in: White Stephen, Pravda Alex and Gitelman Zvi (eds.), *Developments in Russian Politics 5*, Basingstoke: Palgrave, 2001, pp. 269-286.

1. Civic nationalism, with Russian nationhood defined by citizenship of the multiethnic Russian (*Rossiiskoe*) state and loyalty to its key institutions, irrespective of ethnic and cultural provenance.
2. Pure ethnic nationalism, defining Russians (*Russkie*) on the basis of blood ties, a position influenced by the Russian writer Lev Gumilev's vision of Russians as a biological "superethnos".
3. Linguistic nationalism, with "Russians" said to include the thirty million Russian speakers in the former USSR, regardless of place of domicile. However, far from all Russian speakers define themselves as Russian. Even ethnic Russians in the former USSR (some 25 million) often do not define themselves exclusively in ethno-linguistic terms (most evidently in Moldova, where there are more Russian speakers outside the Russian-speaking Transnistrian enclave than within it).
4. Cultural nationalism. "Russians" are defined as a community of eastern Slavs with common culture and origins in Kievan Rus'. This and the former category are heavily influenced by the Slavophiles and usually emphasize Russian Orthodoxy as the bearer of Russian values
5. Statist/Imperial nationalism: these thinkers define the Russian nation as a supranational people with a mission to consolidate former peoples of the USSR or Eurasia within a single multinational state. This approach most clearly approximates to the instrumental Tsarist official nationality and the Soviet approach, and may co-exist with Russo-centrism, particularly of the previous two kinds.

Where have such views appeared in Russian politics? Of all the above views, those espousing civic nationalism have been by far the most politically weak. Although this approach is enshrined in the 1993 constitution (with its view of a multi-ethnic *Rossiiskoe* state) and has been espoused by Westernising members of the political elite (particularly in the early 1990s), it has the weakest intellectual and historical roots in Russia. Furthermore, "Westernisers" are guilty by association with the socio-economic shocks brought on by the first decade of westernising pro-market and pro-democracy "reforms". As Rolf Theen notes, "the crucial nexus between democracy and economic prosperity was destroyed – and with it, the legitimacy of democracy in the minds of the Russian masses".[18] As a consequence, representatives of the other groups have made the political running, and it is they who are usually branded as "nationalists" by analysts. There are dozens, if not hundreds, of

---

See also the much more detailed treatment in Tolz Vera, *Russia*, Arnold: London, 2001.

[18] Theen, "Quo vadis, Russia?", p. 76.

microscopic ultra-nationalist groups with negligible social influence, but we will concentrate only on the major groups here.[19]

Chief among them is the infamous Liberal Democratic Party of Russia (*Liberal'no-demokraticheskaya partiya Rossii*, LDPR) headed by the maverick demagogue Vladimir Zhirinovskii, whose success in Russia's 1993 Duma (parliamentary) elections shocked the world. Opinions differ over Zhirinovskii's platform. It combines fascist and populist "extreme right" elements such as a personality cult, praise of national socialism and dictatorship, and implicit anti–Semitism. We also find Russocentric elements such as militaristic imperialist revanchism and an emphasis on Slavic cultural and linguistic identity, and finally a national liberalism that approves of market economics, civic values and the multiethnic state.[20]

Prima facie, the Communist Party of the Russian Federation (*Kommunisticheskaya partiya Rossiiskoi Federatsii*, KPRF), Russia's largest and most electorally successful political party until the 2003 elections, holds a similar position. The party (particularly its leader Gennadii Zyuganov) mixes a socialist managed-market orientation with claims concerning the cultural–religious uniqueness of Russian Orthodox civilization, the project to re-create a Slavic Union, and protection of Russian speakers abroad. Also it has long sought to ally with Russophile organizations in a succession of "national–patriotic" electoral fronts. The KPRF too is often branded "nationalist", "extreme right", or even "fascist".[21] Yet such labels are problematic: although Zyuganov himself is a national Bolshevik and not an orthodox communist, his position is largely geared toward the broader electorate and is by no means uncritically endorsed by his supporters.[22] Zyuganov's position is it-

---

[19] A good brief overview of such groups, albeit relatively old, is Verkhovsky Alexander, "Ultra-nationalists at the Onset of Putin's Rule" in: *Nationalities Papers*, 2000, vol. 28, no. 4, pp. 707-722.

[20] For a detailed treatment of Zhirinovskii, see Shenfield Stephen, *Russian Fascism: Traditions, Tendencies, Movements*, Armonk: ME Sharpe, 2001, and Devlin Judith, *Slavophiles and Commissars: Enemies of Democracy in Modern Russia*, Basingstoke: Macmillan, 1999.

[21] One such view is Vujacic Veljko, "Gennadiy Zyuganov and the "Third Road"" in: *Post-Soviet Affairs*, 1996, 12/2, pp. 118-154. For detailed analysis of the KPRF's ideological position, see March Luke, *The Communist Party in Post Soviet Russia*, Manchester: Manchester University Press, 2002, chapters 2-4.

[22] See March Luke, "The pragmatic radicalism of Russia's communists" in: Urban J. Barth and Curry J. (eds.), *The Left Transformed: Social Democrats and Neo-Leninists in Central and Eastern Europe*, Lanham MD: Rowman and Littlefield, 2003, pp. 163-208; March L., "The Putin paradigm and the cowering of Russia's Communists" in: Ross C. (ed.), *Russia under Putin*, Manchester: Manchester University Press, 2004, pp. 53-75.

self mutable, and moderate in practice, more *Rossiiskoe* than *Russkoe* (Zyuganov often confuses the two). He typifies the problem of Soviet patriotism – too concerned with ethnic Russians to be truly supranational, and too concerned with the broader empire to be truly nationalist.

The above two parties have made up the backbone of the Russian parliamentary "opposition" (though in practice they have often adopted conciliatory positions) from 1993 to present, while the remainder of the "uncivic" nationalists, particularly those in the extra-parliamentary field, reflect Russian party politics more generally - a plethora of proto-and pseudo-parties, leader-dominated, organizationally and ideologically inchoate, and transient. One of the most commented on was Russian National Unity (*Russkoe natsional'noe edinstvo*, RNE), headed by Aleksandr Barkashov, which espoused "aggressive anti-liberalism, anti-communism and anti-Semitism…ideals of a pure [biological, *author's note*] Russian nation…and Russian spiritual values".[23] It prided itself on its Russian fascism, sported black uniforms with adapted swastikas, armed militias, and militant ethnic nationalism. Yet, despite perhaps twenty-five thousand members and tacit support from some regional leaders, it remained dependent on their whim and never mustered the five per cent support needed to get into parliament, before its final split in 2001, perhaps appearing too extreme and too identified with German Nazi symbolism in the public eye.[24]

The most long-standing ultra-nationalist party is Eduard Limonov's National Bolshevik Party (*Natsional-bol'shevistskaya partiya*, NBP). The NBP is a curiosity. It is obviously fascistic, espousing a Mussolini-style corporatist fascism mixed with a cult of violence and national socialist imagery (epitomised by its symbol, essentially a Nazi flag with a black hammer and sickle replacing the Swastika). However, much of its "fascism" is symbolic, with the party most notorious for propaganda stunts such as the occupation of government buildings and attacks on officials with foodstuffs, while the party (partly in response to state repression) has adopted liberal rhetoric and collaborated with groups such as "Yabloko" at the grass roots level. The party's vivid symbolism and radical style has helped it become one of the most visible among opposition-minded youth, with about 17,500 activists

---

[23] Likhachev V., "Nationalist Radicals in Contemporary Russia: Ideology, Activities, and Relationship to the Authorities" in: *Nationalism, Xenophobia and Intolerance in Contemporary Russia*, Moscow: Moscow Helsinki Group, 2002, pp. 259-282, at p. 262.

[24] See Shenfield, *Russian Fascism*, and Umland Andreas, *Toward an uncivil society? Contextualizing the Decline of post-Soviet Russian Extremely-Right-Wing Parties*, Weatherhead Center for International Affairs Working Paper Series, No. 02-03.

with an average age of 20.[25] However, it still remains a marginal force outside this milieu, especially since Limonov's incarceration from March 2001 on charges of planning terrorist acts and establishing armed militias. The NBP has been continually denied legal registration, and sustained state pressure appears to have stunted its growth.[26] Also highly visible are Russia's 50,000 Skinheads, who have been responsible for savage beatings of foreigners. However, they are not a strongly organised political force. Generally they despise party discipline and ideology, working only as foot soldiers for some of the most aggressively racist groups, such as the People's National Party (NNP), headed by Aleksandr Ivanov-Sukharevskii.[27]

Perhaps the most dynamic nationalist force is *Rodina* (Motherland), the "national-patriotic bloc" founded in September 2003 that stunned observers by getting 9 percent of the Duma vote just three months later. At first view, *Rodina* appears an unstable bloc. It was mainly created as a platform for notable leaders, such as its leading troika, Sergei Glaz'ev, Dmitrii Rogozin and Sergei Baburin, who soon squabbled, leading Rogozin (not noted as a skilled organiser) the sole leader of a diminished party by 2005. It initially benefited from regime support, but once the primary aim of peeling off voters from the communists was achieved, this was less forthcoming (indeed the regime appeared fearful of what they had unleashed). Although its future appeared uncertain, the party had carved out a niche of quasi-left wing "social populism" that may prove popular in future. Indeed, its success is partially analogous to that of newer leftist parties in Europe: the crisis of the old Marxist left, and the populist *Zeitgeist* has given scope for a new "social populism" based on a muting of class politics, electoral flexibility and a quasi-nationalistic populism which champions the deceived "people" (rather than simply the "proletariat") against the corrupt "elite".[28] *Rodina*'s anti-oligarch populism combines with its greater ability (relative to the Communists) to adopt non-left concerns, specifically the ethnic nationalism of its slogan "Russians Must Take Back Russia for Themselves".[29]

Russian Nationalist Support and Influence

The electoral performance of nationalists reflects the fact that their strength

---

[25] *RFE/RL Newsline*, Vol. 9, No. 172, Part I, 12 September 2005.
[26] Likhachev, "Nationalist Radicals in Contemporary Russia".
[27] Ibid., p. 265.
[28] March Luke and Mudde Cas, "What's Left of the Radical Left? The European Radical Left after 1989: Decline *and* Mutation" in: *Comparative European Politics*, April 2005, Vol. 3, No.1, pp. 23-49; Mudde Cas, "The populist *Zeitgeist*" in: *Government & Opposition*, 2004, 39/3, pp. 541-563.
[29] Glasser S. B. and Baker P., "How Nationalist Party Became a Powerhouse" in: *Washington Post*, 15 December 2003, at http://www.washingtonpost.com/.

has been more apparent than real, even when the ambiguously nationalist communists are included (under the term "national-patriotic left"). Indeed a diminution in support for pure nationalists since the high-point of the mid-1990s is visible, with nearly 36% voting for nationalists and the national-patriotic left in 2003 as opposed to 44% in 1995, and no nationalist being successful in presidential elections (see Table 1).

Table 1. National-level electoral support for "nationalists" 1993-2004

ELECTION	NATIONALISTS			NATIONAL- PATRIOTIC LEFT			TOTAL SUPPORT
	LDPR	Others	Total	KPRF	Others	Total	
1993 (Duma)	22.9	-	22.9	12.4	-	12.4	33.3
1995 (Duma)	11.2	8.5	19.7	22.3	1.6	23.9	43.6
1996 (presidential first round)	5.7	14.7	20.4	32.0	-	32.0	52.4
1996 (Presidential second round)	-	-	-	40.3	-	40.3	40.3
1999 Duma	6.0	2.0	8.0	24.3	-	24.3	32.3
2000 (Presidential first round)	2.7	0.4	3.1	29.2	3.1	32.3	35.4
2003 Duma	11.5	2.5	14.0	12.7	9.3	22	36.0
2004 (Presidential first round)	2.0	-	2.0	13.7	4.1	17.8	19.8

Source: author's data

Who votes for the "nationalists"? Despite high levels of voter volatility in Russia, some patterns can be identified. Nationalist voters tend to be from the most economically depressed strata, particularly the young, unemployed (see tables 2 and 3) and from border regions or those with a high ethnic admixture. Nationalist parties such as the LDPR have been able to rely on reserves of support in the institutions most affected by or concerned with Russia's humiliation, chiefly the army and security services. The communists share the nationalist camp's often authoritarian, anti-Western values, but are significantly older, more impoverished and much more nostalgically pro-Soviet. Many nationalists in contrast are almost as anti-communist as they are anti-nationalist.[30] One feature of the 2003 elections was that younger

---

[30] For example, see White Stephen, Rose Richard and McAllister Ian, *How Russia Votes*, Chatham NJ: Chatham House, 1997.

and less impoverished voters could vote nationalist (in particular for the LDPR, as is visible from table 3), and were not automatic liberals, which may be a worrying sign for the future.

Table 2: Household economic situation/Party vote in 2003 Duma election (% within Party vote in Duma election)

		PARTY VOTE IN DUMA ELECTION			
		Rodina	LDPR	KPRF	Total
Household economic situation	Barely make ends meet	12.7%	14.1%	24.8%	15.4%
	Enough for food	38.0%	38.4%	45.0%	37.0%
	Enough for clothes	38.0%	37.4%	24.8%	36.8%
Total	Enough for durables	11.4%	10.1%	5.5%	100.0%

Source: New Russia Barometer XII, 12-22 December 2003, N=1601

Table 3: Age group/Party vote in 2003 Duma election (% within party vote in Duma election)

	PARTY VOTE IN DUMA ELECTION			
Age	Rodina	LDPR	KPRF	Total
18-24	3.8%	19.2%	1.8%	13.7%
25-39	14.1%	31.3%	9.1%	28.5%
40-54	37.2%	38.4%	24.5%	28.7%
55+	44.9%	11.1%	64.5%	29.1%
Total	100.0%	100.0%	100.0%	100.0%

Source: as table 2.

Electoral strength is only one half of the equation however, since Russia's parliament has no direct influence on the composition of government and thereby day-to-day public policy. But there has been a remarkable lack of mass mobilization of ethnic Russians in the extra-parliamentary sphere (frequent but apparently uncoordinated attacks on Jews or ethnic minorities by skinheads, or the stunts of the NBP aside).

Putin and Russian Nationalism

While Russian nationalism has been relatively weak as an organised force to date, this is far from the whole story. Throughout the 1990s, nationalist rhetoric moved from the margins to the mainstream of Russian political discourse. The rhetoric of foreign policy experienced a noticeable shift from the liberal internationalism of El'tsin's first foreign minister Andrei Kozyrev to the assertive pragmatism of his successor Evgenii Primakov.[31] In domestic policy too, Zhirinovskii's success in 1993 was arguably a stimulus to the ill-fated invasion of Chechnya in December 1994, designed precisely to restore some prestige to a humiliated state. More marked still was the "paradigm shift" towards isolationist politics prompted by the August 1998 economic crisis and tensions with the West over its involvement in Iraq and Kosovo.[32] This was reflected in the 1999 elections, where most parties stood on a Russia-first program declaring their patriotic values.

Indeed, Vladimir Putin was a key beneficiary of this playing of the "Russian card", as his domestic legitimacy was forged in the nationalist rhetoric and practice of a re-invigorated Chechen war. Rhetorically the elite indulged in ethnic slander of the worst sort, while a brutal anti-insurgent crackdown in Chechnya led to significant defections from the Zhirinovskii and communist camp during Putin's victory in the 2000 presidential elections.

However, Putin makes a highly ambiguous Russian nationalist, in part because he is more pragmatic than most nationalists, for example by showing a distinct lack of nostalgia for empire in his accommodation of a US forces' presence in Central Asia. He has denounced nationalism and anti-Semitism, called for state efforts against skinheads and other forms of extremism, while he has stressed the civic elements of the constitution, and declared himself "against the restoration of an official Russian state ideology in any form".[33] Nevertheless, other indications are that Putin is a convinced conservative statist-nationalist, albeit of a moderate and pragmatic inclination. For example, in his "Mission statement" of 1999, which arguably is still useful as a distillation of his core beliefs, Putin argues for nationalist shibboleths such as strong statehood, great power status, patriotism and the Russian idea, while adding several at times conflicting conditions, for example:[34]

"Patriotism...is the striving to make one's country better, richer, stronger,

---

[31] See Tuminez Astrid S., *Russian Nationalism since 1856: Ideology and the Making of Foreign Policy*, Lanham, Md.: Rowman and Littlefield, 2000, and Tolz, "Values and the Construction".

[32] Byzov L., "Presidentskaya kampaniya-2000 i novyi electoralnyi zapros" in: McFaul Michael, Petrov Nikolai and Ryabov Andrei (eds.), *Rossiya v izbiratel'nom tsikle 1999-2000 godov* , Moscow: Moscow Carnegie Center, 2000, pp. 484-496.

[33] Putin Vladimir, "Russia at the Turn of the Millennium", Appendix to Putin V. (with Gevorkyan N., Timakova N. and Kolesnikov A.), *First Person: an Astonishingly Frank Self-Portrait by Russia's President Vladimir Putin*, London: Hutchison, 2000.

[34] Ibid.

and happier...free from the tints of nationalist conceit and imperial ambitions." (p. 214)

"I suppose that the new Russian idea will come about as an organic unification of universal general humanitarian values with the traditional Russian values that have stood the test of time." (p. 215)

"Russia will not become a second edition of, say, the U.S. or Britain, where liberal values have deep historic traditions...For Russians, a strong state...is a source of order and main driving force of any change." (p. 214)

This last citation in particular appears to conflict with the preceding one, by implying that liberal values will have no salience in Russia for the foreseeable future if ever. Indeed, Putin appears to believe that a liberal and strong state are antitheses.

In practice, Putin has also demonstrated nationalist overtones that are less moderate. From the outset, he was less careful than Yeltsin with nationalist language, and notably talked of *russkii* patriotism at a Victory Day parade in May 2000. He has promoted Russian Orthodoxy more consistently than Yeltsin, while his own spiritual adviser, Archimandrite Tikhon, is an extreme Russian nationalist. Putin's "patriotism" incorporates both "post-Soviet" and "neo-Soviet" elements that often make it very ambiguous.[35] Under Putin, there has been a definite trend towards a new form of Soviet-era "official nationalism". For example, the re-adoption of Soviet-era symbols such as the national anthem and red military flag preserve continuity with the Soviet period, which (however indirectly) weakens anti-communism and re-legitimises other Sovietesque trends. The 2005 Defence Ministry proposals to create a new *Zvezda* (Star) "patriotic" defence-themed state TV channel, whose goal is to restore love for the motherland in a country whose moral values have allegedly gone astray, are one stark example, the re-appearance of Soviet symbols in adverts and youth fashion another.[36] The Russian government's proposals to introduce a "State Programme for the Patriotic Education of Citizens" aim to re-introduce Soviet style military training in schools and emphasise patriotic sex education in a curious echo of Communist morality and the role of the Komsomol (Communist Youth League).[37]

Similarly, the *éminences grises* of the national-patriotic opposition, such as Aleksandr Prokhanov and Aleksandr Dugin, have lost the pariah status they possessed in the 1990s and become more "establishment" figures, regularly seen or cited in non-opposition media. Dugin in particular

---

[35] Sakwa Richard, *Putin: Russia's Choice*, London: Routledge, 2004, pp. 36-37.
[36] Rostovtseva N., "Moda na levoe" in: *Rodnaya gazeta*, 27 June-3 July 2003.
[37] "Russia launches patriotism drive", www.bbc.co.uk, 19 July 2005.

is regarded as an influential publicist of the anti-Western extreme right among the Russian (especially military) elite, although his views on Russian geopolitics (based around ideas of a global conflict between Atlanticist sea powers ("Thallocracies") and Eurasian land-based powers ("Tellurocracies") are arguably too abstract and fantastic for a mass audience.[38] However, "Patriotic" literature is popular again, with novels by Prokhanov, Eduard Limonov and the more ideological tomes of Sergei Kara-Murza finding an increasing audience.

Of course, the Kremlin, even under Yeltsin, did not shy away from directly fostering nationalist groups as a way of channelling and controlling public opposition. In particular, many have long suspected the LDPR of being a regime stooge whose policy proposals often act as "trial balloons" for Kremlin projects, and which is "a commercial structure ("LDPR-Limited") selling its votes in the Duma".[39] But Putin's greater interventionism has extended into this sphere also, not just with the successful formation of *Rodina*, but with a plethora of pro-Kremlin youth groups, the most recent of which, *Nashi*, or "Our own" has attracted several tens of thousands to rallies. Supervised by Kremlin propagandists such as Vladislav Surkov and Gleb Pavlovskii, it aimed to become a "transmission belt" for regime values to the young, and so insulate the Kremlin from all contingencies in the 2007-8 elections, above all by dominating the streets and suppressing opposition if a disputed election threatened an "Orange scenario". The group took up nationalist themes and techniques, being reputedly linked to football hooligan groups and assaults on opposition activists.[40] Other prominent nationalists have latterly joined the bandwagon of nationalist youth movements, with Aleksandr Dugin in particular seeking to foster a CIS-wide group opposed to the "Orange contagion".[41]

Judging the success of such efforts is premature, but to date, they appear only to have consolidated broader nationalist trends. Putin's statist, centralizing emphasis has appealed to many nationalists, and the defection of formerly nationalist voters to pro-Putin blocs such as "United Russia" means that the electoral strength of nationalist blocs noted above is not in

---

[38] For more on Dugin's influence, see especially, Umland, *Toward an Uncivil Society?*.
[39] Pribylovsky V., "The Attitude of National-Patriots towards Vladimir Putin in the Aftermath of March 26, 2000", from www.panorama.ru", accessed 29 April 2002.
[40] Corwin Julie A., "Is The Kremlin Recruiting Soccer Hooligans?" in: *RFE/RL Russian Political Weekly* Vol. 5, No. 30, 26 September 2005.
[41] Goble Paul, "Window on Eurasia: Eurasians Organize "Anti-Orange" Front in Russia, CIS" in: *Johnson's Russia List*, No. 9242, September 2005.

itself a failsafe indication of nationalist electoral strength. On the whole, Russian or Soviet nationalism has remained largely an elite phenomenon. Nostalgia for the USSR has been combined with little desire to re-create it, while in 1999 the slogan "Russia for the Russians" was supported by only 13-15 per cent of the population, with some 27-32 per cent of respondents considering the slogan to be "fascist".[42] While a civic definition of "Russian" was found to be weaker than a cultural-linguistic counterpart, ethnic self-definitions were also weak. Nevertheless, such sentiments co-existed with significant anti-minority feeling, and more recent polls do accord a far higher prominence to such sentiments, with some recent polls showing the sentiment "Russia for the Russians" to be supported by approximately 56% of population, although there is still evidence of strong internationalist sentiments.[43] Valerii Solovei has confirmed the increasing manifestation of mass nationalist sentiments as a new phenomenon in Russian politics.[44] Arguably, Putin's appeal to images of a strong Russia has created a strong "demand from the top" for nationalism in society.[45]

Russian Nationalism Redux?

We can now synthesise the key factors which have led to the apparent paradox that Russian nationalism is weakly mobilized but politically ubiquitous. Above all, Russia remains beset by weak state-society integration. Russian ethno-political movements need to be seen in the context of the crisis of political movements in Russia *per se*. Civil society institutions that might form the basis for stable parties, such as trade unions, have so far been fragmented and leader-dominated. The lack of ability to organize large-scale extra-parliamentary pressure on the political regime from below deprives political parties of much of their muscle. Against a background of economic crisis and the violent results of the stand-off between president and parliament in 1993 the result has been a marked public political passivity.

---

[42] Data from the All-Russian Center for Public Opinion Research (VTsIOM), cited in Verkhovsky Alexander, "Ultranationalists in Russia at the Beginning of the Year 2000" from www.panorama.ru, accessed 29 April 2002. See also Tolz, "Values and the Construction", particularly pp. 278-280.

[43] This data is from the Levada analytical centre. A VTsIOM survey also showed that 45 percent of ethnic Russians regard their ethnicity as more important than their citizenship. See "Russia for Russians idea gaining support" from Russia Profile (www.russiaprofile.org, August 15, 2005).

[44] Solovei Valerii, "Rozhdenie natsii (Istoricheskii smysl novogo russkogo natsionalizma)" in: *Svobodnaya mysl'*, XXI, 2005.

[45] "Anti-Semitism in Russia. Tendency 2004", from the website of the Informational-Analytical Centre "Sova", www.sova-center.ru, accessed 18 February 2005.

Moreover potentially sympathetic institutions remain either loyal to the state (the church) or divided and demoralized (the army).

While extra-parliamentary groups have withered, a highly corrupt political system that has sought to co-opt political opposition by pressure and payment has compounded party weakness whilst institutional avenues for influencing the executive have been narrow. Parties within state institutions have become increasingly docile. The KPRF's "irreconcilable" opposition has long been thoroughly compromised. Long prior to its 2003 electoral reverse it has become (like the LDPR) repeatedly prone to increasing ideological incoherence and venality. Since they are deprived of strong institutional links between state and society, the exotic theories of elite nationalists are of little help in achieving wider social influence, and the institutionalized anti-liberal social movements that played such a role in paralysing Weimar Germany have not emerged. With their tradition of autonomous military organization, Russia's one million Cossacks might have played an incendiary role akin to nationalist paramilitaries in Serbia, but they are a divided and debilitated force, significantly only contributing to ethnic disturbance under the aegis of nationalistic governors as in Krasnodar and Stavropol. Although Putin has latterly sought to restore the Cossacks to the role of an elite equestrian guard, many observers consider that Stalin's repression of the Cossack movement is an insurmountable obstacle to their future revival.[46]

Overall, personal political rivalries and ideological differences have meant that the Russian nationalist spectrum is a fractured mirror. There are almost as many versions of the Russian idea as parties professing them, differing radically over their attitude to Orthodoxy, communism and political violence. Moreover, they have lacked unifying or effective leadership. Zhirinovskii's personalist, erratic and alternately frightening/comical leadership style alienated many would-be allies, such as the communists, while visceral anti-communism among many nationalists has prevented the emergence of a broad opposition front. *Rodina*'s internal problems may indicate that it will travel a well-trodden road to nowhere.

Regionalization and geographical distance in Russia have compounded problems of identity and organization for all organisations, whether state or non-state. The Russian Orthodox Church was unable to become the backbone of organized national liberation as did the Catholic Church in Poland in the 1980s, while simple poor communications bedevilled social groups from the

---

[46] Parsons Robert, "Russia: Cossack Revival Gathers Momentum" in: *Johnson's Russia List*, No. 9141, 6 May 2005.

outset. Russia's complex federal system has also played a significant role. Russia's twenty-one semi-autonomous national "republics" give formal over-representation to many of Russia's minorities, while excluding some altogether and leaving most of the ethnically Russian population dwelling in administrative regions without a federal relationship to the centre. This remains a potential flashpoint, and indeed many nationalists have proposed to elevate the status of the Russian regions to those of the republics, potentially causing a backlash from the ethnic minorities (leaders of national republics such as Tatarstan have been outspoken in their criticism of anything that smacks of Russo-centrism).

Overall, although nationalists have received official sanction in some areas such as Krasnodar and Stavropol, Moscow has (with the significant exception of the Caucasus) contained local ethnic sentiment, Russian or otherwise. Since Russian politics remains an elite preserve, a series of secretive bilateral treaties was sufficient to palliate regional discontent in the 1990s, whilst recent centralisation means that local political mobilisation is still more circumscribed: since autumn 2004 regional governors are appointed, and legislation since 2000 has made it impossible for groups overtly promoting ethnic, religious or regional interests to organise at national level. Tightened regulations such as complex election registration requirements and the national parliamentary electoral threshold that will move from 5 to 7 percent in the 2007 elections have effectively eliminated the electoral potential for minor nationalist parties such as the RNE and NBP, who consistently failed to get any seats in the national parliament. Indeed, the political elite has, however haphazardly, often sought to defuse Russian nationalism. Gorbachev and Yeltsin generally defined Russian statehood in non-ethnic and non-imperial terms.[47] While Putin is less consistent, it can be argued that the adoption of nationalist rhetoric in domestic and foreign policy has to some degree stolen the thunder of hard-line nationalists, while potentially forging a more pragmatic moderate patriotism.

Finally, the international environment has not been consistently conducive to Russia's nationalist impulses. Moscow's criticisms of Western foreign policy and economic advice are often well-founded, but Russian engagement with international institutions such as NATO and the G8 is still undertaken, even if Russia's relationship with the West appears to be based more on short-term pragmatism than shared interests or values. The thorny issue of the Russian Diaspora has not resulted in an international

---

[47] For example, see Breslauer and Dale, "Boris Yeltsin and the Invention of a Russian Nation-State".

crisis because Moscow has not claimed either the right or duty to interfere (with some notable recent exceptions in Ukraine, Georgian and Moldova). This indicates that Russia knows that greater nationalistic assertion abroad could jeopardise its most valuable international relationships. Indeed, controversial unresolved issues, such as the rights of Russian speakers deprived of citizenship in the Baltic states, have generally been dealt with through diplomatic channels without military or significant economic pressure. Nor has the Russian Diaspora mobilised of its own accord. Even in the Baltics, there is little evidence of threat of direct physical violence to Russians that Rogers Brubaker sees as being important in the politicization of "homeland nationalism" in the diasporas[48], and above all, as noted above, it is far from clear that many "Russians" abroad hanker strongly for their external homeland.

Conclusion

To acknowledge that the full potential of Russian nationalism has been only sporadically and ineffectively mobilized is not to deny that these barriers may not apply in future. Much Russian political discourse shows an elite at best ambivalent about the virtues of a civic nationalism, increasingly insistent on Russia's "special path", and at worst indulging in the manipulation of mass social and ethnic grievances. Putin's Westernising statist nationalism may be the only way to appeal to a nation where liberal and market values are discredited. However, there is a well-known argument democratising states are often more likely even than authoritarian states to promoting nationalist or war-like policies to foster internal consolidation.[49] The weakness of ethnic Russian nationalism is as much a function of its lack of democratic institutionalization as the absence of ethnic and imperial nationalist ideas *per se*. Given this, it seems that even if Russia continues to democratize, it is unlikely that discussion of the Russian idea will abate, and by no means yet certain that a civic version of that idea will prevail.

Moreover, the Kremlin's current attempts to produce and manage an "official nationalism", could, even given the barriers mentioned above, provide fertile ground for the flourishing of mass nationalist sentiments akin to the notorious "Black Hundreds" of the early 1900s, armed squads who

---

[48] Lieven, "The Weakness of Russian Nationalism"; Brubaker Rogers, *Nationalism Reframed: Nationhood and the National Question in the New Europe*, Cambridge: Cambridge University Press, 1996.
[49] Mansfield Edward D. and Snyder Jack, *Electing to Fight: Why Emerging Democracies Go to War*, Cambridge, MA: The MIT Press, 2005.

defended "Tsar, faith and Fatherland" from "the enemy within".[50] Certainly the defeat of the liberal SPS and Yabloko parties in 2003 has contributed to the increasingly nationalistic political climate. Lacking strong support from a diminished liberal intelligentsia, Putin may be tempted to move further towards authoritarian nationalism.[51] On one hand, the governmental United Russia's lack of distinct ideological and leadership profile increases the Kremlin's caution about encouraging a nationalist rival such as *Rodina*, which might in future become a major threat if it escaped regime control. However, the authorities' need to eliminate uncertainties after Putin in the absence of institutionalised popular support may indicate a dangerous temptation. The Russian political system is one characterised by "negative integration".[52] That is, with a distrustful and alienated electorate, it is easier to consolidate support by mobilising against an "other" than it is through positive appeals to such things as governing competence, and party programmatic appeal, which have not always existed in the post-Soviet era. The Russian presidency has always needed an "other" against which to define itself: such a role was played by the communists in 1996, the Chechens in 2000, and the "opposition" in 2004. The temptation for the presidency to rely on nationalistic, "anti-Orange" or even anti-Western appeals in 2008 will be strong.

---

[50] Hosking, *Russia and the Russians*, p. 344.
[51] Smith M. A., "Putin's Nationalist Challenge", Conflict Studies Research Centre, Russian Series 05/20, May 2005.
[52] White, Rose and McAllister, *How Russia Votes*.

FEDERALISM IN RUSSIA: OUTCOMES OF THE DECADE 1993 - 2003 AND THE NEWEST DEVELOPMENTS

Irina Busygina

In Russia as well as in other countries in transition, where federalism has been chosen as the organising principle of political relations between the centre and the regions, federalism in itself represents a special and extremely important dimension of transition. The basics of the federal order were created under President Yeltsin. However, some urgent problems were not addressed. Moreover, the federal order developed with severe distortions during the 1990s. The era of President Putin started with reforms of the relations between the centre and periphery. New institutions were created, while other institutions' roles in Russia's political system changed. The "new" federation acquired a much more centralised character. The political role of regional elites decreased drastically. During his second term, President Putin continued to reform Russia's federalism. The main innovation was the abolishment of the direct elections of governors. This was a step backwards, not only for federalism, but for the democratisation process as a whole. Another issue, which is currently propagated heavily by the federal centre as an important direction for reforms in the country's statehood, is the enlargement of federal subjects. The underdeveloped system of political parties in Russia, which has not yet acquired an "integrated" character, is another important factor restricting the development of Russia's federal order.

Outcomes of the Decade 1993-2003

The federal order in Russia was built in the beginning of the 1990s by "unconscious design". We say "designed" because its main institutions were constructed "from above", artificially – they did not grow out of pre-existing political practices. However, this design was unconscious because the functions of these institutions and the rules of the game were not determined by a systemic approach and a clear vision of strategic goals, but primarily by the particular political momentum (our politicians would argue that it "proceeded from political advisability").

The Federation Treaty of March 1992 was the first document that tried to shape new, federal-style relations between the centre and the regions. In the first place, the document intended to diminish the threat of territorial disintegration in the new Russian state. Additionally, according to the Treaty, all regions received the status of constituent entities (subjects of the federation[1]). At the same time the document established the asymmetric character of the federation, whereby the subjects were divided into four types: (1) republics, (2) *kraya, oblasti* and cities of federal subordination, (3) autonomous districts and (4) autonomous *oblasti*. In this complicated system the republics have been granted more rights and competences than the other regions.

In 1993, when the political crisis in Russia was solved through unconstitutional means, the federal centre (*in casu*, the President) increased its influence. On 12 December 1993 the new Constitution was adopted by referendum. This document has seriously strengthened the institution of the Russian Presidency and laid the base for federal relations in the country. However, it did not solve some urgent pre-existent problems. *To begin with*, there was the problem of equal status for all subjects of the federation. Article 5 of the Constitution declares the principle of equal status for all subjects, but other articles of this document stress that their status is not equal. Hence, the text of the Constitution is contradictory and this generates constant tension between the republics and the other regions. *Secondly*, the Constitution does not solve the so-called *matryoshka* paradox: seven subjects of the federation *(kraya* and *oblasti)* contain nine other subjects (autonomous districts). The Constitution avoids the problem through Article 66, which grants the subjects the right to find their own solutions. However, even the Constitutional Court was not able to find a convenient solution to this problem.

In spite of the fact that the federative relations in Russia were to some extent shaped through institutions and legislation, they remained unstable and lacked clear mechanisms. The instability showed itself in three main aspects: the extremely complicated structure of the federation and its asymmetric character; the gigantic disproportionality between the regions in terms of regional per capita product, size of territory, population and economic profile; the weakness of the federal centre, which until 1999 had lost nearly all means of influencing the situation in the regions. The policy of the federal centre towards the regions was generally *ad hoc*, determined by short-term political, economic, ethnic or even (and often) personal factors. The "Yeltsin federation" thus had "weak legs". Its transformation towards a more centralised union or a loose confederation was only a matter of time.

---

[1] In the Soviet Constitution of 1977 only ethnic republics were listed as subjects of the Russian Socialist Federated Soviet Republic (RSFSR).

During the nineties, President Yeltsin tried to build his relations with the regions via a system of exclusivity, the development of political favouritism and personal bargaining. Informal institutions and rules of the game began to either replace the new formal institutions or to fill the existing institutional vacuum. Federalism in Russia did not acquire the value of a public good. It remained federalism "from above", designed according to the political situation. Not only did the population not treasure federalism, it did not perceive the federal order as a public good. Federalism did not contribute to democratisation in the regions; on the contrary, in many, authoritarian political regimes began to grow.

This situation generated a new mood in society – from enthusiasm to disappointment over federalism, which was seen as "not fulfilling its promises" (promises which, incidentally, were never given). The necessity of reforms became obvious. Various versions of federal reforms – from constitutional to administrative – were discussed in academic circles. The reality proved to be faster and simpler; the reform of the federation was realised by President Putin and his team.

It should be mentioned here that already in 1999 two processes had started developing in Russia. At the federal level, there was a strengthening of the "power block" (the so-called *siloviki*), a process that started when Sergei Stepashin was nominated Prime Minister. At the regional level, there were attempts to shape regional political blocks; the most prominent examples are *Otechestvo* (Fatherland) of the Moscow mayor Luzhkov and *Vsya Rossiaya* (Whole Russia) headed by the President of the Republic of Tatarstan, Shaimiev. Later these forces united into a "regional coalition". However, it had little chance of survival and its quick capitulation was predictable: *firstly,* the coalition was not internally stable as its leaders had different goals (Luzhkov had presidential ambitions while Shaimiev wished to defend his Republic's political autonomy); *secondly,* the coalition could not expand because its leaders focused only on the rich regions, while most of the Russian regions were heavily dependent on subsidies from the federal centre. The coalition not only capitulated, but it also clarified itself as the primary danger to and "enemy" of the main actor.

The reforms introduced by the new President entailed several aspects and included a whole package of documents. The main elements of the reforms were:
– The creation of seven federal districts and the nomination of Presidential Representatives;
– The institution of federal intervention;
– The reform of the Federation Council.

The Presidential Decree on the formation of seven federal districts was the first step of the reforms[2]. The Decree tried to solve the problem of co-ordinating the various federal agencies working in a region[3]. Their efficiency was very weak and often depended on the regional executive power, which *de facto* "privatised" them. In many regions, the federal structures did not act in the interests of the federal centre, but in the interests of the regional establishment[4]. Thus, the Decree represented an attempt to separate the federal agencies in the regions from the regional executive powers, and to increase the presence of the President in the regions. President Putin broke with previous practice whereby Yeltsin built his support in the regions on the personal loyalty of the governors and personalised his relations with them. Putin created a new institution between the President and the governors.

Experts and analysts are divided in their opinions about the meaning of this new institution. Some are inclined to examine it very seriously, as a "unitary superstructure over the federation"[5], while others see in it as a "purely technological rationalisation"[6]. I would not overestimate this political innovation: it was directed towards a new organisation of the federal agencies in the regions, but did not seek to reform (at least formally) the system of state power in general.

The institution of federal intervention is defined by the federal law – "On changing the federal law 'On the general principles of organisation of the legislative and executive bodies of state power of the subjects of the Russian Federation'" – adopted by the State Duma on 19 July 2000. The initial federal law was adopted by the Duma only in October 1999. This was extremely significant for the regions. The law had been sidelined for years – first by the President, then by the Federation Council. However, the law neither foresaw the creation of an institution of federal intervention nor established the responsibility of the regional bodies. In other words, the law of October 1999 is the best argument to the thesis that, toward the end of the Yeltsin era, the federal centre had practically no mechanisms for influencing the situation in the regions.

---

[2] Decree N°849 "On Representatives of the President of Russian Federation in the Federal District",13 May 2000.

[3] These are the regional agencies of the Ministries of Foreign Affairs, the Tax Service, the Tax Police, Domestic Affairs, Defense, etc. In total, more than 380,000 people work in these regional agencies.

[4] See Smirnyagin L., "Wonderful Seven" in: *Russian Regional Bulletin*, May 2000, 2/10, p.22.

[5] See Zubov V., "Unitarianism or Federalism (To the Question of Future Organization of Russia's State Expanse)" in: *POLIS*, 2000, N°5, p.32.

[6] See Kaspe S., "To Construct a Federation – *Renovatio Imperii* as a Method of Social Engineering" in: *POLIS*, 2000, N°5, p.67.

The new federal law ("On changing the federal law 'On the general principles of organization of the legislative and executive bodies of state power of the subjects of the Russian Federation'") had to improve the situation. The new law foresaw:
- the responsibility of the regional state power bodies in the case of a violation of the federal Constitution or the federal legislation;
- the capacity of the President to dismiss, (after approval of the Duma) the regional legislature
- the ability to dismiss the head of the executive power of a region by Presidential decree in the case that this regional executive issued a law or a legal act contradicting the federal Constitution or the federal legislation;
- the capacity of the President to dismiss the head of the executive power of a region if the latter were accused by the General Prosecutor.

Thus, this law tried to fill in the gaps of the previous law.

In fact, the institution of federal intervention is a common feature that corresponds with a federal order. The law in general (along with the federal districts) increased the presence of the federal centre in the regions and decreased the status of the governors, changing drastically the whole logic of the development that took place in the previous period. In this respect, I consider the political will of the President to be justified insofar as it aimed at preventing the further consolidation of the authoritarian regional political regimes, which also prospered because of the weakness of civil society structures in the regions.

The Federation Council or, as it is called in Russia, the "collective voice of the regions" is a rather peculiar institution. During its short history, the principle for forming this institution changed three times[7]. Indeed, in December 1993 the deputies of this body were directly elected by the population (two from every federal subject); in 1995 after long discussions the principle was changed and the heads of the regional legislative and executive branches of power received their mandates without elections. Finally, in July 2000, a federal law was adopted, according to which two representatives from each federal subject form the Federation Council – one from the legislative branch and one from the executive. The representative of the legislature is elected by regional deputies, while the representative of the executive branch is nominated by the governor unless two thirds of the legislature votes against this candidate.

---

[7] Art.95 of the Constitution does not elaborate on the principle of the formation of the Federation Council.

Since 1995 the Federation Council has displayed a lot of pragmatism, orienting itself toward consensus rather than towards confrontation with the President. V. Ryzhkov called this body a "political stabilizer". In addition to this, the Federation Council has become a kind of political school for regional leaders and a means through which they move to the national level of politics.

After the reform of 2000, the new Federation Council, composed of regional representatives, no longer corresponded with the constitutional objectives of this body because these deputies have no political weight and their names are new on Russia's political scene. Thus, the new formation principle of the Federal Council entails the weakening of parliamentarianism in Russia, that is a decreased parliamentary role in the division of power. Second, the new principle clearly shows the real meaning of the reforms: to push the governors away from the Council and to take away their immunity as deputies. In this context, the reform was undertaken according to the same logic as the introduction of the federal institution of intervention.

The first results of the innovation have already appeared. We observe not only the atomisation of the Federation Council, but its transformation into a lobbying body. The deputies have been turned into political managers employed by the regional executive and legislative bodies: the governor can easily dismiss his political employees.

A brief summary of the elements of the Putin's administrative reforms is shown in the table below, comparing the main features of the "Yeltsin" and "Putin" federations.

FEATURES	YELTSIN	PUTIN
1. Character of relations with the regions	exclusive, political favouritism	"equalisation"
2. Support for the President in the regions	governors	representatives in federal districts
3. Institution of federal intervention	no	yes
4. Political status of the governors	high	low
5. Political status of the Federation Council	(relatively) high	(relatively) low, shared with State Council
6. Formal/ Informal Institutions	dominant informal institutions	dominant formal institutions
7. Responsibility of regional/local authorities	no	yes

As a result, the regional leaders were in clear need of some sort of compensation. The most important compensation was the creation of a new body – the State Council. This was meant to be a "political body of strategic importance". The range of the problems discussed at the Presidium of the Council (composed of seven governors nominated by the President, one from every federal district, to be replaced each half a year by others, according to a rotation principle) shock the imagination: strategic planning, hymn and heraldic, etc. However, the nature of the issues discussed is relatively unimportant as the Council has only an *advisory* status. President Yeltsin, acting within his competences, created the advisory Presidential Council, composed of the "most wise and respected" people of the country whose political weight was close or equal to zero. President Putin, also acting within his competency, has decided to create another advisory body in order to compensate the governors for their loss of political status. The magazine "Itogy" has called the Council "the factory of governors' dreams"[8] which is, perhaps, close to the truth.

In general, the institutional federative system in the Russian Federation was shaped under President Yeltsin. However, the system not only inherited some "black spots" from the Soviet period but also developed in a distorted way during the 1990s. Therefore, a reform of Russian federalism was needed. Regarding the character of the reforms we can make the following observations. The reforms have acquired a feature of irreversibleness. The legislative shaping of the reforms was done extremely fast. The reform had an "aggressive" character, driven by the President and his team. This was possible due to a new situation of no confrontation between the President and the Parliament (with the consequence that the role of the latter as an independent actor in the political process obviously decreased). The reforms were not discussed in Russian society, but were undertaken through administrative pressure. In other words, the President did not feel the necessity to discuss his intentions with society.

The character of the reform was not constitutional but administrative. However, the capacity of the administration was notably broad: a lot was achieved without altering the Constitution. The reforms preserved the institutions, but changed their substance, their interaction, and the rules of their game. The reforms proved that the institutions as political structures were created in Russia, but their functioning and political weight could still be the object of political experimentation.

It would be quite difficult and probably counter-productive to evaluate

---

[8] See *Itogy*, November 28, 2000.

the reforms in positive or negative terms as they contained different elements. However, the basic sense of the whole reform was not more centralisation but the destruction of the system of federative relations built under President Yeltsin. The reforms drastically changed the existing model of centre-periphery relations. Interestingly, the previous system lacked supporters; neither political parties, nor regional elites, nor society in general were eager to defend the "Yeltsin federation". The experts now tend to write that "we have to gradually abandon federalism, as it is inadequate for Russia", that "federalism as a organisational principle of Russia's political space does not have a solid historical basis"[9], etc.

The character of the reforms reflected in particular the President's vision of federalism, which consisted in "strengthening the vertical power structure". In this vision federalism is perceived as a set of certain technical operations related to the delimitation of competences between the federal and regional levels of power but not penetrating into society. The reforms sought more formalisation with regard to the functioning of the institutions, but, paradoxically, the opposite has been the case – the institutions grew more informal internally, becoming more like political lobbies (the Federation Council is a good example).

One of the strategic goals of the reforms was to weaken the regional elites (firstly, the governors)[10] and to concentrate the resources (administrative and financial) in the hands of the federal bureaucracy. Regional elites as well as oligarchs have vacated the federal political scene. This was, however, only one objective. Another objective seems to be aimed at transforming the federal bureaucracy into a locomotive which would provide economic growth at any price. Thus the "Yeltsin federation" has been sacrificed for economic growth and administrative reform should not be examined only in and of itself, but also as a means to create a framework for economic growth.

The model of federalism was to be national: it should correspond to national statehood in general. As a political principle it is a product of national statehood and of its development. The second term of President Putin corresponds to the second wave of reforms of federalism in Russia.

"Soft Nomination" of Governors

Until 1990 the heads of the regional executive authorities were not elected by the population but nominated by Moscow. From 1991, after the proclamation

---
[9] See, Zubov, o.c., p. 54; Kaspe, o.c., p. 55, *POLIS*, N°5, 2000.
[10] The President stressed that "there were, are and will be no special relations between the Kremlin and the governors" (*Nezavisimaya Gazeta*, 29.09.2000).

of sovereignties, the republics started to elect their own presidents. This practice was soon copied by the other regions. Consequently, the first three heads of the regions were elected at the same time as the President of Russia: the mayors of Moscow and Saint Petersburg (G. Popov and A. Sobchak, respectively) and the President of Tatarstan, M. Shaimiev. The "second wave" of gubernatorial elections started at the same time as parliamentary elections – President Yeltsin allowed them to be conducted in 12 regions. It should be mentioned that during these elections the incumbents had enormous resources – the administrative "machines" and regional mass media worked for their campaigns. The last nominated governor remained in the Kemerovo oblast, until elections in this region took place in October 1997. After this time, all the governors in Russia's regions were *directly elected*.

Direct elections created a new relational situation between the federal centre and the regions since, for the first time the heads of the regions received direct legitimation through election rather than nomination. Nevertheless, the elections proceeded with serious deviations from democratic norms. In some regions there was a clear trend towards the degradation of democratic procedures through a consolidation of the regional elites. The elections showed the power of administrative "machines" in the regions and, at the same time, a serious failure of the federal centre. The main condition for preserving a governor's authority was not his or her loyalty to the centre but support from the regional elite. The elections contributed to an increasing consolidation of the elites in the regions and increased the degree of their "closeness"[11].

In the regions mono-centric power systems started to take shape (a so-called quasi-presidential form of government), with the governor at the top of this system. The regional elite turned into autonomous subjects of the political process. This trend corresponded to the process of political regionalisation in Russia, i.e. moving the centre of the decision-making process from Moscow to the regions. The governor became the *political leader* of his region[12]. However, the formation of the gubernatorial body – as an autonomous subject of politics at the national level that would defend certain "regional interests" – did not happen (this also explains why the "regional coalition" surrendered) because of the intensity of the power struggle. The governors did not have a leader who would be recognised by the majority – the chairman of the Federation Council, E. Stroev, the mayor

---

[11] N. Petrov and A. Titkov. "*Vybory glav ispolnitel'noi vlasti regionov*". In *Vybory i partii v regionakh Rossii*. M-SPb, 2000, pp.72-74.

[12] R. Turovsky. *Politicheskaya geographiya*. Moscow-Smolensk, 1999, pp.260-261.

of Moscow, Y. Luzhkov, and the governor of Sverdlovsk oblast, E. Rossel, tried to act as leaders.

From the year 2000 the elections of governors proceeded in a totally different political context: the new President strengthened the "vertical power", he changed the relations between the federal centre and the regions, and he introduced a new institution – the federal districts. The elections of 2000-2002 were very tense. A new phenomenon was the flow of "alien" figures, especially from Moscow, to the regions, who actively took part in the election campaigns. The regional leaders showed an extremely high degree of loyalty towards the federal centre, first of all to the President. None of the serious candidates expressed opposition to the presidential policy line. In fact, support for the President and/or for the political party *Edinaya Rossiya* (One Russia) became the main political means to achieve victory in the elections. The federal centre thus became a new and powerful factor of influence in the regional political process.

The second term of President Putin is the time for further centralisation and for broadening the field of federal intervention. On 13 September 2004 the President put forward some new initiatives during a session of the federal government that were presented as instruments to fight terrorism. A need for a system of "soft nomination" of the governors was proclaimed (and later realized through federal law). According to this new system, after being nominated by the President, the governor is not elected directly by the population but by the regional legislature. The President has to choose one candidate from a list prepared by his representative in the federal district to which the region belongs. If the regional legislature rejects the candidate for governor three times, the President *has the right to dissolve the legislature and nominate the head of the region by (his) decree.* After the adoption of the new federal law, all regional parliaments had to re-write their regional charters, removing the statement concerning the election of the governor.

It should be specially mentioned that such a mechanism is not used in any other federative polity in the world. Yes, there are governors in such federations as Canada or India who are nominated by the federal centre, but they *only* represent the interests of the centre towards the subjects of the federation, while the functions of the governing executive are concentrated in the hands of elected political figures (the prime minister – the leader of the political party that won the regional election campaign).

The abolishment of direct elections of governors clearly marks a step backward – not only for federalism in Russia, but for the whole democratisation process as well. The regional leader has lost his or her status as the legitimate representative of the executive authority in the region.

Such a procedure goes against the federal Constitution and the federal laws. The governor has also lost his position as political leader, becoming a sort of manager of his region instead. The "soft nomination" of governors is in fact a powerful instrument of federal intervention. To date (the new rule has been applied in 32 regions), not one candidate of the President has been rejected by the regional legislatures.

At the end of September 2004, the regional legislature of Yaroslavskaya oblast decided to address the Constitutional Court to request an interpretation whether this new procedure was in accordance with the law (this was the second protest – the first was sent to the Court in June by 17 members of SPS[13]). After the elections of 2004 the parliament of this particular region was one of the very few where *Edinaya Rossiya* did not obtain a majority. However, the governor of Yaroslavskaya oblast had already determined the decision as a "non-consequent policy and desire to produce political scandal"[14].

Territorial Reform

A federation is a living organism – it always seeks to find better balance between centripetal and centrifugal forces. Consequently, no one can completely determine its characteristics (in particular the territorial structure, or the number of constituent entities). The development of modern federations shows that in principle the creation of new federation subjects is more frequent than the enlargement or merger of subjects. Changes in territorial structure can occur in a young federation (for example, Nigeria) as well as in mature and stable ones (here the best example would be Switzerland). Modern federations also differ enormously with one another in regard to the mechanisms of territorial reform: in the Indian federation it is very easy to change the territorial structure, as the decision has only to be taken by the lower Chamber of the national Parliament. In Germany, however, the process is extremely difficult: it starts from a referendum and should end with the approval of a qualified majority in both chambers (the *Bundestag* and the *Bundesrat*). In my view, the general approach on territorial reform is the following: the territorial structure of a federation should be changed *only* in the most necessary and urgent cases when the intensity of internal conflicts reaches a very high degree.

In Russia the issue of territorial reform – decreasing the number of constituent entities – became the most popular topic related to the further de-

---

[13] SPS is the Union of the Rightist Forces, a liberal political party.
[14] *Vedomosti*, 29.09.05, p.A2

velopment of Russian federalism. Most of the Russian territorial units do not have a long history as they were created during the 1920s and '30s. During Soviet history one could observe waves of territorial reforms – "waves of mergers were replaced by waves of splits". Since 1957 the administrative territorial division of Russia (at that time the RSFSR) did not change until 1991, when the regions, due to the legal chaos of that period, strengthened their administrative status unilaterally – autonomous republics were transformed into republics (with the exception of the Jewish autonomous republic) and autonomous districts were detached from the regions to which they previously belonged. This process became known as the "parade of sovereignties".

The territorial structure of the "new" Russia was already a topic of political debate before the new Constitution was adopted in 1993. At that time there were three main scenarios for reform: (1) restoration of the pre-revolution "*gubernii* order" (a symmetric federation without ethnic divisions); (2) a symmetric federation consisting of Russian regions and national republics; (3) national republics and one huge Russian republic, which would embrace all the territories populated primarily by ethnic Russians. However, none of these scenarios were feasible – such a profound reform would immediately lead to a severe crisis and to the political collapse of the country.

The ideas of territorial reform were revived at the beginning of Putin's second term in office and the idea gained popularity rather quickly. The federal executive authority, first and foremost the main political actor, President Putin, presented the reform – the enlargement of the regions – as an innovation generated by the population and in the interest of the population. The idea was also supported by some governors; in the autumn of 2000 the governors of the Sakhalin, Saratov and Yaroslavl regions proposed a decrease in the number of "superfluous" subjects of the Russian Federation. In 2001 the State Duma adopted the federal law "On the acceptance into the Russian Federation and the establishment of a new subject within the Federation". At that moment there were plenty of reform plans which would reduce the number of regions to 15, 28, 50, or 70.

As for the theoretical background of the reform, the basic approach had (and has) a so called "objectivist" character. In other words, the territorial division should be based upon certain objective factors such as geography (the borders of a region should correspond to "natural" borders) or economy (a region should represent a full economic complex). In my view this "objective" approach (in particular, its economic dimension) represents the remnants of the old Soviet idea of territorial-productive complexes that is unrelated to territorial divisions within a federation.

On the contrary, it would be very dangerous to create "full", self-sufficient regions as it could lead to fragmentation. A situation where entities have many different kinds of borders that *do not correspond but cross* each other provides a more stable and integrated scenario. The idea of framing economic life into administrative borders corresponds to a country with a state-controlled economy, but Russia pretends to be a country with a market economy where the economic "life" and the administrative "life" proceed separately. However, the official Russian ideology of territorial reform is based primarily on economic grounds, the idea of creating self-sufficient economic regions. Additionally, the proponents of the reform support other arguments according to which the reform would mean the better management of territories, less bureaucracy, less asymmetry within the federation, all of which would eventually solve "the national problem". However, none of these statements had any serious evidence. During the propaganda campaign launched by regional and federal authorities these statements were taken for granted.

It was clear from the beginning that once the territorial reform was launched, it would start from the *matryoshka* regions and would first touch small and economically weak autonomous districts. The unification of the rich Perm region and the small and weak Komi-Permyak autonomous district (KPAD) – a territory inhabited by only 150 thousand people and depending heavily on federal donations – was chosen to be a "pilot" project to test the mechanism of unification. This explains why the federal and regional authorities did their best to minimise the risks during the process. The unification started with a referendum in both territories that showed positive results (84% for unification in the Perm region and more than 90% in KPAD). In February 2003 the governor of the Perm region and the head of the administration of KPAD signed an agreement and a memorandum on the creation of a new subject of the Russian Federation: both documents were then sent to the President. In July 2005 President Putin signed the federal law to create a new subject of the federation – Perm kraj. The law was adopted by the State Duma (17 June) and by the Federation Council (22 June). The new subject of the federation – Perm kraj –started functioning from 31 January 2005.

During this first process of unification the federal centre tried to solve several problems simultaneously: to guarantee a minimum level of autonomy to KPAD after unification, to present the unification as a *regional initiative*, and to calm the elites from the other regions who observed the process of unification. Not only did the President actively support the idea of unification but, by his decree, he provided significant compensations to KPAD in order to solve the most pressing issues: supplying gas to all KPAD settlements until 2006 as well as the construction of a bridge across the Kama River and roads connecting the remote territories of KPAD. In addition, the President promised that until 2008, KPAD would continue to receive full donations from the federal budget – that is, more than one bln. roubles per year. It should also be added that this first successful unification had another consequence – the federal Constitution needed to be changed for the first time since 1993

Unification in the Urals can be considered as a kind of prelude to unifications that would touch the richest of Russia's regions, the *matryoshka* regions – Krasnoyarsk kray (which should be unified with the Taimyr and Evenk autonomous districts) and Tuymen oblast (to be unified with Khanty-Mansi (KhMAD) and Yamalo-Nenetz (YaNAD) autonomous districts). The reason for unifying Krasnoyarsk kray and its districts is related to the aluminium, nickel and coal industries. Moreover, there is an area rich in oil and gas on the territory of the kray. These huge territories are very rich in natural resources, but not densely populated. The idea of unification did not cause protests; the referendum in the region showed positive results[15] and afterwards according to normative procedure the federal law was adopted by the Federal Assembly and signed by the President.[16]

However, the case of the "large" Tyumen region is, in my opinion, totally different. First of all, this is a key region for Russia as it guarantees Russia's export of oil and gas. Oil resources are concentrated on the territory of KhMAD, while gas resources are located in the North, in YaNAD. These are territories where the interests of the largest Russian oil and gas companies (such as Lukoil, Surgutnefregas, TNK, Sibneft, Rosneft) are concentrated. As for Tyumen region itself, it has no outstanding resources; it is a "normal" region on the border of Kazakhstan with some agriculture and manufacturing. Both autonomous districts have significant populations: 1,250,000 in KhMAD and 500,000 in YaNAD. Both territories have developed legislation, social policies and infrastructure, and thus the districts are more developed than the Tuymen oblast. From this perspective, the idea of unifying them with the Tuymen region does not sound reasonable. It would be more rational to increase their status to that of *oblast* rather than

---

[15] In Krasnoyarsk kray the decision about unification was approved by 92,4 %, in Taimyr autonomous district – by 69,9%, in Evenk autonomous district – by 79,9% (Institute of regional politics, http://regionalistica.ru/monitoring/rotation/referendum/).

[16] Federal Constitutional law, 14.10.2005 № 6-FCL, text available at the official web-site of the President of Russian Federation: http://document.kremlin.ru/doc.asp?ID=030005

decreasing it. Additionally, when considering the geography, it is obvious that this unification is extremely dangerous. The new subject would stretch from the South to the North of Russia – from Kazakhstan to the ocean – thus creating a great "hole" in the country's territorial structure separating the European area from the Asian area (Siberia and the Far East). Such a territorial entity would concentrate almost all of Russia's exports and could therefore demand special political relations with Moscow.

In the spring of 2005, the process of merger started in the Far East; in May the heads of administration of the Kamchatka oblast and the Koryak autonomous district signed a protocol on their intention to create one region that would embrace their territories. On 23 October 2005 a referendum took place and the majority voted for the enlargement. The adoption of federal law by the Federal Assembly, signed by the President in July 2006, confirmed the unification of these two "poor" regions that heavily depend upon federal subsidies.[17]

In general we can conclude that the Russian Federation really has an enormous number of territorial units and its structure is asymmetrical. I believe that reforms in this field are needed. Not only economic reasons justify reforms, however, but also the fact that some territories (in particular those with thinly populated districts) have *no opportunities to develop into real political communities*. In these cases reforms should not necessarily result in unification. It would be much more reasonable to turn these districts into "federal territories" without the status of subjects of the federation. Such an approach is more flexible regarding the future development of the districts. Nevertheless, even if unification is adopted as the basis of territorial reform, it should not change the orientation of state building. It should become a state policy or a political instrument and political campaign of the federal centre. In every case merger should take an *individual approach* (for example, the leaders of some republics in the Northern Caucasus already predict severe inter-ethnic conflicts in case of fusion). The lack of revision or the ability to unmake a unified territory should also be considered, since the federal Constitution does not foresee the fragmentation of unified regions in the future.

Federalism and Political Parties in Russia

In 1953 the famous explorer of federations Kenneth Wheare wrote: "Here is a factor of the organization of federal government which is of primary

---

[17] Federal constitutional law, 12.07.2006, №2- FCL, text available at the official web-site of the President of Russian Federation: http://document.kremlin.ru/doc.asp?ID=034659

importance but which can not be ensured or provided for in a constitution – a good party system"[18]. Today's researchers of federalism write about *integrated parties* (or an integrated party system) which represents one of the most significant conditions for preserving federal stability. In such a system politicians at one level of government bear an organisational relationship to politicians at the other levels. The relations between both levels (national and regional) are generally close. Authors writing on federalism identify some specific criteria of an integrated party: the existence of the party's organisation at all levels – national, regional and local; the party's electoral success at the national level facilitates electoral success at the other levels; the party regional and local organisations retain sufficient autonomy[19]. Integrated parties unite the country and prevent it from fragmenting. On the other hand, the capacity of regional party entities to control centralisation impulses, guarantees "federal freedoms". A political party in a federation is not a Lenin-type construction made of "steel", but a loose and flexible structure; the flexibility does not weaken, but strengthens the federal order. If we look, for example, at Germany, we will see that its party system generally exhibits these characteristics. The German party system is almost the same at the federal level and at the *Länder* level (with the exception of Bavaria). Regional party organisations follow the national guidelines with some deviations due to the particularities of a region. The candidate nomination process is controlled by local and *Länder* party organisations.

The Russian Federation represents a completely different picture. The formation of political parties from the end of the 1980s to the beginning of the '90s developed extremely a-synchronically at national and regional levels. At that time, the centres of party building, besides Moscow, were large industrial cities with developed democratic movements: Saint Petersburg, Yekaterinburg, Novosibirsk, Yaroslavl, etc. However, the activities of the national political parties in the regions were far from sufficient. The only exception was the KPRF[20], which was represented in all regions. The so-called party of power – *Nash Dom Rossiya* [Our House Russia] of the 1990s – existed primarily in the form of candidate lists, prepared by regional administrations. Liberal parties like *Yabloko* and later SPS did not feel the necessity to "conquer" the regions.

For this reason, national political parties and blocks paid little attention to the election of regional legislatures (again with the exception of the KPRF). In 1995-1997, the average number of "party deputies" at the regional level was

---

[18] Wheare K., *Federal Government*, London: Oxford University Press, 1953, p.86.
[19] Filippov M., Ordeshook P., Shvetsova O., *Designing Federalism*, Cambridge: Cambridge University Press, 2004, p.192.
[20] KPRF = the Communist Party of the Russian Federation

18.9% of the total[21]. Candidates to the post of governor tried to escape from official affiliation with one party in order to widen their potential "election field". (This "non-party" affiliation of the regional leaders is one possible explanation for the absence of one recognised leader among the governors. It is also why a regional leader has no chance in Russia to immediately have a career at the national level – for example, to be elected as President, as it can happen in the USA or Germany where the regional politician represents not only his territory but at the same time a national political party). At the end of the 1990s the weakening and degradation of party structures and their marginalisation became obvious at the regional level.

As one of the priorities of the political reforms after 2000, the federal authority proclaimed it would increase the role of political parties. As a result, the federal law "On political parties" was adopted in 2002. This document stated that no less than half of the deputies of regional legislatures should be elected according to a proportional system. It also destroyed the phenomenon of regional parties in Russia as it stated that a political party should have its affiliations in not less than 50% of the regions. Consequently, only members of national parties could take part in regional elections. The election results of the regional legislative assemblies of 2003-2005 show that in the majority of the regions the factions of *Edinaya Rossiya* (Kaluzhskaya, Chitinskaya, Vologodskaya and Sverdlovskaya oblasti, Tatarstan, Kalmykia, Mordovia, etc.) dominated the parliaments. In some cases the "party of power" shares its majority with a faction of the KPRF (Vladimirskaya, Sakhalinskaya and Volgogradskaya oblasti, etc.) or with *Rodina* (Voronezhskaya and Yaroslavaskaya oblasti).

Another political innovation – the introduction of the proportional system for the State Duma – will also necessarily have some consequences for the Russian federal order. Some of this system resembles a unitarian state model more than a federation[22]. Taking into account the nature of political parties in contemporary Russia (those without an integrated character), requiring the parties to compose the State Duma seems absolutely non-reasonable or at least premature. All Russian parties perceive federalism, in the best case, as a burden[23] and the State Duma is traditionally oriented in a "unitarian" way due to the fact that the Duma parties do not have roots in the regions. One of the consequences of the introduction of a new election system is not difficult to predict: the further weakening of regional representation in the lower chamber of the Federal Assembly.

---

[21] Luchterhandt-Michaleva G., "Izbiratel'ny process i partii v rossijskikh regionach" in: *Vybory i partii v regionach Rossii*, M – SPb, 2000, p.144.

[22] See Zakharov A., "Izbiratel'naya sistema i dukh federalisma" in: *Obshaya Tetrad*, Moscow, N°2 (33), 2005, pp.51-58.

[23] Filippov et al., *o.c.*, p.312.

Federalism and Society

Federalism is not only a set of technical decisions of how to delimit competencies between the federal centre and the constituent units, nor even a matter of a political principle. In order to survive and flourish a federal order requires special societal conditions. In my opinion, these special conditions could be analysed through three main dimensions.

1. International experience shows that a federal order has tremendous difficulties to survive in poor or vertically fragmented societies – that is, in societies where large gaps in the level of income and quality of life exist between social groups. Poor societies cannot "allow" federalism as it is too complicated and too expensive a system. In cases of severe vertical disparities, federalism develops either through a series of conflicts between social groups (e.g., Nigeria) or becomes increasingly centralised insofar as state presence (or even state violence) is needed to govern society (e.g., Latin American federations, especially Venezuela).

In Russia, one can clearly observe a huge and growing discrepancy between the country's geographic size and its currently negligible economic and trade weight, as well as its low "social status" among the nations of the world[24]. If one takes into consideration social indicators (quality of life, life expectancy, infant mortality, etc.), Russia is definitively a society with very low social standards. Moreover, vertical fragmentation (the gap between rich and poor) has show a visible and growing trend over the last years. Thus, the recent re-centralisation and retreat from the previous mode of relations between the federal centre and the regions could be explained (at least partially) by the necessities for holding together a disintegrating society.

2. Federal order presupposes the prevalence within the society of a certain type of political culture. This should be, obviously, a civic culture which is based on a two-sided process: the state issues norms and decisions, while the population has real channels and opportunities to influence the decision-making process. This should also be a "federalist" culture with a public consensus on such values as mutual trust, tolerance, the ability to reach compromises and to conduct negotiations.

In Russia, these values are not yet popular within the political class nor within society at large. The current political culture in Russia is extremely heterogeneous. It is a mixture of many different strata. One of its main characteristics is state paternalism combined, paradoxically, with an

---

[24] See Trenin D., *The End of Eurasia. Russia on the Border between Geopolitics and Globalization*, Washington D.C.: Carnegie Endowment, 2002, p.11.

expressed distrust of institutions of power. Contemporary Russia is a society of distrust. In addition, it is a "society of divisions" of various dimensions – between East and West, North and South, city and countryside, centre and periphery, etc.

3. Real federalism defends not only group and territorial, but also private interests. Talking about "federalism", we would immediately notice that there is a brilliant set of political essays including not only a hymn to the de-concentration of power, but also lauding private property[25]. Those who have property should govern the country – this is the focus of a "federalist" philosophy. It is obvious that the one completes the other. A de-concentration of political power means that strong institutions in the regions correspond to the interests of this class of owners and that the owners live everywhere across the country.

In Russia, we observe a lack of interest in federalism as (in my opinion) a consequence of the absence of a middle class in the regions (or the absence of a *critical mass* of those belonging to the middle class). The middle class is the social group that would have property in the regions and, for this practical reason, would wish to determine their region's political and economic agenda and would compete for political positions under democratic rules.

Some Conclusions

The basics of the federal system in Russia were built during the 1990s (more precisely, from 1992 to 1997). However, some of the urgent problems, either inherited from the Soviet period or created by the *ad hoc* policy of the federal centre, were left unsolved. Federalism in Russia was not a stable order, but was constructed from "above" and did not acquire the value of a public good – the population remained indifferent towards this issue. The "regional coalition" that was shaped at the end of the 1990s had no opportunities to influence the new political regime that began to take shape in the country at the same time.

The reforms of President Putin during his first years had a multi-dimensional character and included such important elements as the creation of seven federal districts, the introduction of federal intervention and the reform of the Federation Council. The reforms either constructed new institutions or preserved existing ones while changing their substance and the character of their interrelations. As a result, the previous model of centre-regional relations changed profoundly; in particular, the reforms reflected

---

[25] See *Federalist. Political Essays of A.Hamilton, J.Madison and J.Jay*, Wesleyan University Press: Middletown, Connecticut, 1961 (See Art.7, 37, 44, 85).

the perception of federalism by the federal executive authority. Federalism was perceived as a set of purely technical mechanisms. Not only did the reforms weaken the regional elites, but they removed them (as well as the oligarchs) from the federal political scene. Thus, the "ruling coalition" became very narrow in comparison with that of Yeltsin's term.

The most important innovation of the second term of President Putin was abolishing direct elections of regional governors, who consequently lost their status as political leaders, and turned them into regional managers. This represented not only a step backwards for federalism in Russia, but for the democratisation process as well. The most popular issue now is the merger of the federation's constituent entities. This process progressed very quickly and passed from being a "regional initiative – made by the population and for the population" – to a "normal" federal policy. It should be added here that the arguments "for" merger have never been explained by federal and regional elites who dare not to resist. The political party system in Russia – put forward by the centre as a priority – does not yet stimulate the development of federalism and the last innovations (a new electoral system for regional and federal parliaments) look even less promising in this respect.

Federations are extremely different from each other because federalism is a flexible order that allows different institutional designs. But this wide "field" of federalism is definitely not endless; at a certain point the political system moves (maybe unintentionally) from the group of federal polities to the group of (decentralised) unitary ones. I believe that Russia has already made this crucial move – from a self-declared, decentralised federation to a centralised one – and onwards even to a *de facto* decentralised unitary state with (remaining) a federalist rhetoric, but without the comprehensive institutions needed in a federation and without the "spirit of federalism".

THE RUSSIAN PARLIAMENT AND VLADIMIR PUTIN'S PRESIDENCY

Andrei Zakharov

Analysing the Russian political system is at the same time easy and difficult. The problem is easy to solve insofar as the core feature of the Russian political system at present is its mono-subject-ness and, hence, simplicity; the Russian political arena is a one-man stage for a solo performance. In structural terms, Putin's mono-centrism is much less complicated than was Yeltsin's. There are currently no political forces in the country that are capable of talking with the President as an equal, and, hence, the political landscape is extremely primitive.

At the same time, making this analysis is difficult because the Russian "elective autocracy" can by no means be considered predetermined nor is its bright future ensured. Over the past six years, the voices of those who believe that the political system of Russia is on the threshold of a serious crisis have grown increasingly loud. Sceptics declare that the primary factor of the looming crisis is that the current regime lacks a political alternative.

The Yeltsin Regime

In order to understand the essence of Vladimir Putin's regime, it is necessary to describe, at least briefly, Boris Yeltsin's legacy that Putin inherited. In his effort to reconstruct the communist state permeated with the communist party ideology, newly independent Russia's first president purposefully stimulated political pluralism and the decentralisation of power. Attempts were made by fits and starts throughout Yeltsin's entire tenure to embed the principles of a separation of powers, political competition and turning an idea of civil society into social practice. Even when unable *de facto* to carry out his administrative duties during his second term as president, Yeltsin continued to zealously uphold the freedom of the press. However, while recognising Yeltsin's merits, it is necessary to point out that, as a whole, the system he was building, as with any other transition system, remained crossbred and internally inconsistent. Probably its main (though not the only) contradiction was a combination of personified authority and a democratic mode of legitimation.

In the 1990s, Russia became a typical non-liberal democracy[1], which

---

[1] Zakaria F., *The Future of Freedom: Illiberal Democracy at Home and Abroad*, New York: W.W. Norton, 2003.

means that elections were held on a regular basis, but the decision-making processes within the political structures which those elections made legitimate were most often not liberal in spirit. Russia had serious problems with human rights, excessive government intervention in all spheres of social life, and maintaining the supremacy of law. The principles of separation of powers and independent courts were adhered to, but only incompletely and selectively. The level of the population's alienation from the government institutions kept rising, which caused a special headache for the representative bodies of power; suffice it to recall that since the middle of the 1990s, the level of trust in both houses of Parliament has seldom exceeded ten percent.

For all that, the development of authoritarian trends, which were no doubt close to the heart of Yeltsin as the head of state, was contained by several systemic factors[2]. *First of all,* the presidential authority was checked and balanced by the other branches of power. During Yeltsin's reign, the legislative branch of power grew increasingly mature as an institution and acted as the centre for the opposition. Additionally, the judiciary, especially the Constitutional Court, repeatedly claimed greater independence. *Secondly,* the Russian regions and their democratically elected heads acted as a powerful counterbalance to the Kremlin in the 1990s, when they became aware of the benefits of federalism and began to use the upper house of Parliament – the Federation Council – as the main tribunal for upholding their interests. *Thirdly,* the regime was forced to maintain an equilibrium between various oligarchic lobbies in an effort to balance the interests of one against another. *Fourthly,* inside his inner circle, Yeltsin tried to make the rival groupings – the "liberals" and the *siloviki* – toe the line. *Lastly,* it was impossible to ignore the rapidly evolving civil society, which was capable of bringing measurable pressure upon the government from time to time.

The combination of these factors resulted in the end of violence being a core tool of state policy. Strong opposition, both right- and left-wing, appeared in Russian society in the middle of the 1990s and its political activities grew increasingly well-ordered in character. The scale of state intervention in public life was shrinking considerably.

All of the above, however, failed to eliminate the fundamental contradictions inherent in Yeltsin's Russia. By the end of his presidency it had become obvious that *the President's efforts to beef up his own authority failed to strengthen the state; on the contrary, they weakened it,* as they made the destiny of the whole system dependent on one of its elements. Besides this, Russian society had no resources for the maintenance of absolute power,

---

[2] Shevtsova L., *Yeltsin's Russia: Myths and Reality,* Washington, D.C.: Brookings Institution, 1999.

since autocracy can only be effectively ensured through complete reliance on violence, and the use of violence was not popular in post-communist Russia. Meanwhile, the system faced its most serious challenge: a weak government had to carry out economic liberalisation, a process during which *the economic development requirements worked against the consolidation of democratic principles.* But Yeltsin's autocracy was unable to make a resolute choice in favour of authoritarianism. The impasse resulted in a stagnation of the Russian political system.

The Putin Regime
Before Yeltsin's resignation, political scientists spoke about three possible scenarios for the country's political future: a) continued stagnation, b) consolidated authoritarian tendencies, and c) further democratisation. The choice made by the first President of Russia in naming his successor and securing his ascent to power ensured the implementation of not one, but two scenarios: a combination of variants a) and b), that is of continued stagnation against the background of consolidated authoritarian tendencies. Now that Putin has served the larger part of his term as allowed by the Constitution, this conclusion can hardly be called into question. The most graphic feature of the "authoritarian stagnation" in the system of government is the rise and consolidation of the institution of presidential authority, while the other state institutions – first of all, the Parliament and courts – have receded into the background.

Putin came to power under the slogan "Consolidation of Order". The popularity of this slogan with the electorate is easy to explain: under Yeltsin the state developed so clumsily that its intervention was unnecessarily excessive in some instances and negligent when the government should have been more active. The deficiency of public control over the government generated numerous abuses, which irritated the voting community. In the economy, the need for order led to a desire to curb the activity of oligarchs who aspired to play a bigger role in the country's political life.

While modifying the regime, Putin left the omnipotence of the President inviolably towering above society, not answerable to it. The executive branch of power became the fulcrum for building Putin's "vertical subordination system", a hierarchy in which all the other branches of power were subordinate. Widely popular among the Russian ruling elite was an idea of "freezing" the legislature for the duration of economic reforms; the judiciary was also put under effective control.

Symptomatic in this context are the metamorphoses which Russian federalism has experienced under Putin. In this area the President carried out a number of important reforms. *First*, seven federal districts, never mentioned in the Constitution, were created to streamline the activity of the federal bureaucracy in the regions. Each federal district is headed by the President's plenipotentiary representative who plays the key role in the appointment of the regional chief executives. *Secondly*, the Federation Council, or the upper house of Russian Parliament, was reformed. Under Yeltsin, each territory delegated its governor and regional Parliamentary chairman to the Russian Senate; under Putin the regional heads were stripped of this right and were instructed to appoint to the Federation Council one representative of the regional executive and one of the regional legislature. Certainly, as a result of this move, the political resources at the disposal of the regional heads for bargaining with the federal centre were dramatically reduced. *Thirdly*, a massive campaign was launched to bring the regional constitutions into conformity with the Constitution of the Russian Federation. In the preceding years, significant divergences existed, which at times had the capacity to threaten Russia's territorial integrity. This dangerous tendency climaxed in a demand by the President of Tatarstan that the Russian federal Constitution be brought into line with the constitution of his republic. *Fourthly*, federal intervention was institutionalised to allow the centre to take over when a regional governor failed to be efficient, for example, due to serious economic miscalculations. *Fifthly*, the practice of free public elections of the regional administrative heads was abolished. Now the regional heads are practically appointed by the President, who nominates someone from a list compiled by his representative to the federal district who is then considered by the regional legislative assembly. *Finally*, the election system was reformed; as a result, representation of territorial constituencies has disappeared from the Federal Assembly's lower house, or the State Duma, to be replaced by the election of all Duma deputies on party tickets. Simultaneously, the regional parliaments also switched to electing 50 percent of their deputies on a party basis.

There are many arguments in favour of each of these changes. Each change was called upon to put an end to negative practices that loosened state efficiency and ran counter to the very spirit of federalism. The cumulative result of all these actions, however, was the formation of a system that has little or nothing in common with federalism, a system resting on the maximum *concentration* of power, whereas decentralisation, a division of powers, is the basis of any genuine federalist polity.

The President and the Parliament

The 2004 presidential elections resulted in legitimating a regime which was described by Russian political scientist Lilia Shevtsova as *a bureaucratic authoritarian* regime. Its basic components, Shevtsova notes, are as follows: a) power is personified and the leader towers above society; b) the leader leans on bureaucracy and the army; c) society is depoliticised; d) the government includes technocrats who carry out reforms; e) western monopolies participate in the development of the economy[3].

The system's short-term advantages are primarily a result of high oil prices, which enable it to effectively patch up any social tears. The regime still enjoys enthusiastic support from the Russian citizens who were sick and tired of Yeltsin's incapacity and believed that the young and vigorous leader (Putin) promised a fresh beginning. The new democratic nomenclature shaped during the Yeltsin period assisted the new President because it expected him to keep and consolidate the emerging new bureaucracy. However, these factors were quite fickle; aware of this fragility, the new policy makers paid special attention to the consolidation of its pillar – *the institution of one-man authority*. It should be noted that they have made considerable headway in this direction over the past five years: the opposition has been pacified, freedom of the press has become limited, and civil society has been bridled. As a result, the only figure still active on the chessboard of Russian politics is the President, whose political uniqueness, according to some analysts, guarantees unprecedented stability in the country.

What place is Parliament assigned in the system described above? First of all, the Federal Assembly certainly is not an institution capable of exercising serious influence on government policy. According to the 1993 Constitution, all political and economic priorities in Russia are outlined and realised not by the Federal Assembly but by the President and the cabinet controlled and directed by him. Almost all levers of influence in the executive at the disposal of the Duma members have a purely emblematic value. Impeachment of the head of state stipulated by the Constitution is practically unrealisable. Since the President has a right to fill blanks in the legislation with decrees, the deputies cannot feel confident even when acting in the field of law-making. Even when the State Duma passes a vote of no confidence in the government, it does not lead to an automatic resignation of the cabinet; the last word remains with the head of state. When assessing the work done by the Russian deputies, one involuntarily recollects Anatole France's words about the French Third Republic: "I forgive the republic for its bad governance as it controlled and directed almost nothing".

---

[3] Shevtsova L., *Putin's Russia*, Washington, D.C.: Carnegie Endowment for International Peace, 2005 (2nd ed.).

However, all of this does not mean that the Federal Assembly is completely barred from decision-making[4]. Over the last few years, up to the time of the reform that removed the regional heads from the upper chamber, the Federation Council played an appreciable role in streamlining federal relations and teaching the Kremlin the intricate art of reaching agreements with the regions. The lower house, or the State Duma, for its part, reflected the national line-up of political parties and became a sort of barometer of the voters' preferences. Meanwhile, parliamentary election campaigns have gained the status of "primaries" ahead of presidential election campaigns. This, the 1999 Duma elections clearly demonstrated, as they essentially predetermined the outcome of the struggle for the post of president of Russia by provoking disarray in the anti-Putin coalition headed by Luzhkov and Primakov.

What is the Russian Parliament like today? Since Putin has occupied the key position in Russian politics, the State Duma has been elected twice – in 1999 and 2003. Inherent in its present configuration is a range of certain internal features. These include specific *contradictions*, which have matured due to particular institutional factors. Moreover, each of these contradictions determines to some extent the development of the lower house of Parliament. A list of these specific contradictions is as follows:

- "Putin's" State Duma, unlike the two preceding "Yeltsin" convocations, has a majority capable of securing the promulgation of liberal economic acts. However, this majority has no *ideology*, as it brings together forces lacking a properly articulated ideological programme. The only clearly formulated programme priority of the lower house members is "support for presidential policy".

- The State Duma's "efficiency rate" is currently *the highest* in the history of its existence – this is made clear by the overall number of acts passed as well as a drastic reduction in the number of laws vetoed by the President. As compared with the previous convocations, it is necessary to admit, however, that its influence over state affairs is *the lowest*, as evidenced, in particular, by (1) the recent establishment of a new consultative body with vague competences (the Public Chamber, alongside the Parliament) and (2) an abrupt decrease in the law-making activity of the deputies.

- The lower house's United Russia faction, which backs Putin, controls *not simply an absolute*, but a *constitutional* majority, enabling it to get the State Duma's approval on any decision it makes. United Russia

---

[4] Remington T.F., *The Russian Parliament: Institutional Evolution in a Transitional Regime, 1989-1999*, New Haven & London: Yale University Press, 2001.

representatives lead all the State Duma committees and make up the majority in the Duma Council that coordinates all business done by the lower house, even though just over one third of the country's voters cast ballots in favour of the United Russia party in the last general elections.

- One of the rules of the parliamentary game played by the United Russia faction is the almost unconditional approval of any action undertaken by the presidential administration while launching continuous attacks on the government, which is actually formed by the President and pursues his policy line. As it is, the Federal Assembly is hardly involved in any classical functions of law-making, representation or control over the executive branch of power.

This situation that has developed inside the lower house can be regarded as a natural result of its recent evolution. Let us deal primarily with the causes for the disappearance of the Duma's previous ideological reference points, which shaped its activities.

In the early 1990s approximately one-third of the electorate in parliamentary elections voted in favour of the Communist Party of the Russian Federation, which enabled the party's powerful representation in the lower house. At this point, the leftwing opposition launched a process to penetrate all power structures. By incorporating the most actively discontented forces, the 1993 Parliament was able to substantially decrease the degree of political confrontation in the country. Indeed, the smooth functioning of the State Duma, undisturbed by any dissolutions in the wake of its creation, symbolised in the best possible way the existence of a national political consensus over Yeltsin's Constitution and the rules of the game set forth in it. By the end of the 1990s, none of the serious political actors had an interest in toppling the regime: for all of them, without exception, the benefits of political bargaining and observance of the institutionalised rules outweighed any benefits to be gained by breaking the rules.

Yeltsin's painless transfer of authority to a successor at the end of 1999 meant, *inter alia*, that *the struggle against communism ceased to be a priority* for the Russian political elite. This issue was believed to have been finally resolved. As a result, parliamentary politics grew more prosy and boring before our very eyes. The State Duma is now engaged in making decisions not so much on the destiny of one or another ideology but on the political survival of various segments of the political elite. In this context, the career-making stimuli of factional activity have, undoubtedly, overcome any ideological motivations.

Taking these developments into account, it is pertinent again to address the prime characteristic of the current State Duma. With regard to the ideological deficiency in a majority of the Duma factions, we can observe that, of the main factions, only the Communist Party of the Russian Federation can claim certain ideological attributes (in the traditional sense of this word). The other associations (United Russia, Motherland and the LDPR) have no such "burden" to bear. It is not at all a question of these deputies lacking ideological preferences or partiality; no doubt, most of the members of Parliament have their preferences in this field, but they are too amorphous and elastic.

Any valuating judgment about this fact is obsolete at this point. The current state of affairs is neither good nor bad; it should be examined as a natural stage in the development of the Russian Parliamentarianism caused by the logic of Putin's presidency. The new paradigm that prevails between the Kremlin administration and the Duma deputies *does not presume any* political clarity of principles and guidelines, such as those declared by supporters of the Kremlin in the State Duma. As President Putin is himself a politician given to understatements, his supporters among the deputies also are compelled to appear "colourless". It should be admitted that they have succeeded rather well in their efforts; no other Parliament in the new Russia has been so "dull" and "featureless". The present structure of the lower house is fundamentally cheerless; there are practically no interesting personalities in it and those few "long-livers" whose manners or eloquence featured prominently in the preceding convocations have actually receded into the background, putting up with the new rules of the game. To some extent, however, this specific characteristic enabled the last two convocations of the State Duma to project a variety of images to the public, depending on the situation. It could appear liberal and reformist when discussing IMF recommendations, nationalist while debating the union with Belarus, and moderately conservative in its analysis of the issues facing the Russian education system.

Moreover, in a parliamentary life, "boredom" is a phenomenon that is more positive than negative. If the Duma proceedings become uninteresting to watch on television or read about in a newspaper, it only means one thing: the lower house of Parliament has finally become a "tool" or "machine" which does not need colourful figures for it to function normally. The existence of a "stable majority" in the State Duma makes it possible for the presidential administration to supervise quite effectively the law-making activity in the house. Since almost everything that the executive branch of power initiates is immediately supported by a majority, a relationship of "intimate consent" has emerged between the Parliament and the President.

Parliamentary Efficiency

The last convocations of the State Duma have been extraordinarily effective from the functional point of view, as evidenced convincingly by a comparison of the parameters of the Duma's legislative activity. Thus, during its first convocation (1994-1995), about one in every four laws passed by the deputies was vetoed by the President. As regards the bills passed by the Duma's second convocation (1996-1999), the President disagreed in 17 percent of all cases. As for the last two, "Putin-era" convocations, instances of presidential veto or return of passed laws to the house without consideration have become extremely rare – a mere five percent of the total number of the acts passed by the Duma.

Additionally, since the above-mentioned radical "revamping" of the Federation Council, it has become more appeasing in its relations with the lower house; the passage of bills through the "corridors" and "faction rooms" of the Russian legislature has become even smoother. The statistics on presidential decrees show the same regularity. First, their frequency has decreased considerably over the past few years and, secondly, it is especially noticeable that there are fewer presidential decrees on economic matters, as this segment of the legal field is better regulated by Parliament's laws. When the people's deputies cope with their duties efficiently, there is simply no need for rule by decree.

Certainly, the numbers do not tell the whole story. To be fair, it is necessary to say that over the past years the Federal Assembly helped to revive some major legislative initiatives. A list of major bills that were completely blocked by the previous deputies, but were recovered by their successors, is extensive and continues to grow. In this context it is sufficient to mention the Land Code, the Labour Code, the Criminal Procedure Code, and the packages of laws designed to reform the courts and reconstruct the pension system. All things considered, observers are unanimous that the current State Duma has been working consistently and without failure to fulfil a liberal legal and economic agenda as approved by the country's top executive.

Despite the above-listed achievements, the lower house is growing increasingly weaker as an institution. One telling symptom of this trend is that the sources of initiative for the State Duma increasingly originate beyond its own walls. Before 2001 the Duma deputies initiated more than half of all bills, but in 2001 a symbolic boundary was crossed: the President and the government outstripped the members of Parliament in law-making by raising more than 60 percent of all bills for consideration in the lower house.

Analysts note repeatedly that in the present conditions rarely does the lower house refuse any bill if the executive authority insists on its passage. This hypertrophied law-making activity of the Kremlin and the Russian White House is inherently paradoxical. In countries with parliamentary governments (i.e. the cabinet structure depends directly upon the will of Parliament), the executive authority is usually inclined to monopolise the process of fixing legislation. For example, in Canada or in the United Kingdom it is extremely rare that an individual MP introduces a new draft law. The indisputable explanation for this fact is that within the "Westminster model" the government is a sort of outgrowth of Parliament and represents its dominant majority. Consequently, it is compelled to engage in legislative work.

In Russia, the situation is quite different. Any attempts by deputies to introduce pro-parliamentary principles into the political life of the country (the best-known attempt of this sort was undertaken during Yevgeny Primakov's short-lived premiership) have been resolutely quashed by the executive branch. Putin's inheritance from Yeltsin restricts him from completing the traditions of his presidential autocracy. Indeed, a decisive step in this direction would require constitutional changes because the minor status of Parliament is a basic principle of the Constitution.

Unwillingness to control

It seems that the tendency of "the executive's" growing activity in the legislative field will continue. In other words, the independence of the Parliament from the other bodies of government, which is an unmistakable attribute of its institutional maturity, is becoming less and less noticeable in Russia. In the context of the entire post-communist period, one could note a certain current *recoil, a return to the past*. Instead of growing complexity in the political system, which would testify to the evolution of the democratic system, its *simplification* is observable in Russia. A problem is Parliament's fundamental vulnerability due to its externally derived inspiration and energy. According to the Russian press, the "Putin phenomenon" is at the core of this problem: all trust is placed in him alone and not in the institutions of governance that translate his policy into practice. The majority of citizens, according to sociological surveys, think, first, that the State Duma and the Federation Council are engaged in unnecessary activities and, second, that the dominant position of the United Russia faction in the State Duma is legitimate, given the President's popularity. The faction and party will feel secure in this position only, however, if the Presidential team succeeds in pulling the country out of the current economic and political crisis. Putin's first serious failures could dramatically alter the line-up of forces in the State

Duma, threatening not only the well-being of the pro-Kremlin factions but also the prestige of the house as a whole.

The previously described situation is explained to a considerable degree by the *absence of a genuine multi-party system in Russia*. Indeed, almost all of the Russian parties are either pre-election projects or elite groupings known only in Moscow and lacking support structures in the regions. The Kremlin recently expressed its concern in this respect by tightening the requirements for political parties seeking official registration; they are required to increase their membership, to be active across the federation, instead of limiting their activity to a limited number of regions, etc. At the same time, however, the government painstakingly refrains from taking the most logical step toward strengthening the parties; the latter are still not trusted with the formation of the government. What is the outcome? Deprived of the opportunity to translate their slogans and programs into practical activity, the Russian parties lack stimuli for engaging in real competition. They decide nothing and nothing depends on them; the President continues to nominate candidates for prime minister and he is the only one able to dismiss heads of government. The absence of political competition severely curtails the Parliament's capacity as an institution of power as well as any competition between the parties. Hence, the Duma factions are fake, a puppet show.

A transformation of the representative bodies of power into an executively wielded instrument is believed by some to be only a temporary guarantee for consolidating political will. According to classical theories of modernisation, reforms are carried out most successfully when the number of political actors is purposefully reduced to a minimum. To agree with such a scenario would, however, imply that the members of Parliament are not granted any control over the actions of the executive. In the meantime, a government left in a political vacuum is capable of making very serious mistakes.

Conclusions

Based on the above discussion, some conclusions can be made about the place of the Russian Parliament within the political system constructed by Vladimir Putin. *First* and predictably, the emergence of an absolute pro-presidential majority in the lower house has not brought about any increase in its political authority. On the contrary, the opposite is true: the State Duma is losing its identity as an institution of power. *Secondly*, there are no hopeful signs of an improvement in the Parliament's position within the constitutional system since certain external forces – the President and the government – have surely enhanced their role as the prime initiators of the Duma's activities. In other words, the current Parliament is extremely weak and deprived of independence and it will most likely remain weak and dependent in the foreseeable future. *Thirdly*, the "instrumental" approach to legislative activity is one of the numerous manifestations of *the technocratic principle* which is so fashionable now in the ruling circles of Russia.

Thus, as has repeatedly happened in Russia's domestic history, "things basic" are again being sacrificed in favour of "things transient". While striving to achieve economic growth at any cost, the country sustains inevitable losses. It is sad that young Russian Parliamentarianism is soon to appear on the mournful list of these losses.

CONCLUSION :
ELUSIVE RUSSIA ? HOW TO UNDERSTAND TODAY'S RUSSIA ?

Katlijn Malfliet and Ria Laenen

Why is it so difficult to find a common language with Russia? Through the sequence of EU-Russia summits in the framework of the Partnership and Cooperation Agreement the disillusion of the European Union became difficult to hide. Even if the European Union sees its relationship with Russia as a "pragmatic partnership", trying to retain the dialogue and to seek progress through positive incentives rather than negative sanctions and punitive measures. And even if the European Union strongly believes in its peaceful image as a civilian power, Russia remains difficult to understand as a partner.

How can we come to a strategic partnership with the Russian Federation when this partner is increasingly difficult to talk with, and when it is so difficult to unveil its real face? How can we speak of common spaces if Russia claims its own understandings of values and norms? EU-Russian relations surely do not develop in the direction of a cooperation based on commonalitry and trust. On the contrary, the dialogue becomes more suspicious and sharp, as has become illustrated recently in the EU-Russia energy dialogue.

Of course it is not only Russia that changed its position towards the West. The West itself, especially the European Union fell into a deep crisis of values and norms. The European Union got stuck in a process of defining its political identity in a new constitutional treaty. In most cases Russia is right when it criticises the so called "double standards" of the West. The European Union's human rights concept is indeed not always flawlessly linked with minority policies and citizenship protection. But on the other hand Russia is certainly not without guilt in the deaf ear's dialogue between Russia and the West.

The state of affairs offered in this volume does focus on Russia's domestic reforms and developments. All authors in this volume agree that Russia changed enormously during this decade and a half of its independent existence with regard to its state paradigm, national concept, and federal relations. Implicitly, each of them expresses some degree of disappointment over the outcome of the transition process, because the hopes for a democratic federation with a working parliament or a clear national identity for the multicultural Russia is almost gone.

After the demise of the Soviet Union we saw a Russia appearing under Yeltsin, eager to integrate in the West, calling itself democratic, and ready to re-define itself as a nation and a federation. At this moment the self-definition of Russia has changed tremendously. A new national patriotism has emerged, and as Luke March emphasizes: it is a top down nationalism.

Russia does not make it easy for us, the observers, to get to a basic understanding of its national idea. However, some contours of a new Russian idea are taking shape, both in official and broader circles. One of the Kremlin's main ideologues Vladislav Surkov comes up with a concept where a certain form of national patriotism can be detected.[1] Without doubt also the idea of social justice will figure prominently in the concept of Russia. The new national idea will serve the aim of opposing to the West, formulating a mission for Russia in line with Russia's historic self-claimed role as having a *mission civilatrice*, creating a we-feeling that is not based on a concept of ethnic nationalism.

Now that Russia defines itself in terms of a democracy under the Rule of Law, a modern federation and a multicultural nation-state, the question remains: What does Russia understand under these terms? Clearly not the same as we do: it is a question of semiotics, of de Saussure's "sous-entendu". The political analist Vitali Tretyakov claims for example that the foreign term "sovereignty", should be replaced by its Russian analogue: "autocracy" *(samoderzhavie)*, i.e. the desire and ability to independently define one's own destiny and rules of life in one's society. Thus a doctrine of "sovereign democracy" is launched, which can be defined as "autocratic self-government" *(samoderzhavnoe samoupravlenie)*.

On the World Congress for Russian People in April 2006, sponsored by the Orthodox Church, Metropolitan Kyrill, who is in charge of the external and international relations of the Russian Orthodox Church, casted some doubt on the universally applicable character of the Universal Declaration of Human Rights.

We entered a new era in Russian politics, one that hopefully is also transitional. We should not come to forgone conclusions about Russia's future. As long as Russia finds itself "Between Dictatorship and Democracy" as has been concluded by some leading Russia experts, there is still hope that the current development is only a temporary deviation along the trajectory

---

[1] Lipman Masha, "Putin's "Sovereign Democracy"" in: *Washington Post,* July 15, 2006, accessed at http://www.carnegieendowment.org/publications/index.cfm?fa=view&id=18540

followed by post-Soviet Russia. A policy of disengagement from the West would steer Russia only further away from the path towards full-term liberal democracy. Academic research on Russia and an open dialogue among academics from both Russia and the West should remain a primary objective. Having started out with common values and the metaphor of the "Common European Home", at the moment the risk is realistic to end up after 15 years with count Sergei Ivanov's famous triad, designed to philosophically prop the conservative and anti-Western regime of Nicolas I. This simply cannot be the end of the story...

ABOUT THE AUTHORS

Irina **BUSYGINA** is Professor and Director of the Center for Regional Political Studies at MGIMO at the School of Political Science of MGIMO (Moscow). Professor Busygina's research focuses on Russian and German federalism, center-periphery relations from the Russian and European perspective, regional identity and regional policy. Her publications include "Federalism and Administrative Reform by President Putin the Context of Democratic Transition in Russia" in *The Concept of Russia: Patterns for Political Development in the Russian Federation* (ed. by K. Malfliet and F. Scharpé, Leuven University Press, 2003), "Russian Regional Institutions in the Context of Globalization and Regionalization" in *Explaining Post-Soviet Patchworks* (ed. by K. Sebers, Aldershot, 2001); Концептуальные основы европейского регионализма. //В кн.: Регионы и регионализм в странах Запада и России. - М., 2001; Стратегии европейских регионов как ответ на вызовы интеграции и глобализации. М., Интердиалект, 2003.

Luke **MARCH** is Lecturer in Soviet and Post-Soviet Politics at the University of Edinburgh. He spent much of the late 1990s working on the communist left in the former USSR, in particular its ideological and organisational development and influence on democratisation. Recent publications include 'Virtual Parties in a Virtual World', in Sarah Oates, Diana Owen and Rachel Gibson (eds.), *Civil Society, Politics and the Internet.* (Frank Cass, 2005); 'Russian Parties and the Political Internet', *Europe-Asia Studies*, vol. 56, no. 4, May 2004; 'The Putin paradigm and the cowering of Russia's communists' in Cameron Ross (ed.), *Russian Politics under Putin* (Manchester University Press, 2004); 'The Pragmatic Radicalism of Russia's Communists', in Joan Barth Urban and Jane Curry (eds.), *The Left Transformed: Social Democrats and Neo-Leninists in Central and Eastern Europe*, (Rowman and Littlefield, 2003) and *The Communist Party in Post-Soviet Russia*, (Manchester University Press, 2002).

Marie **MENDRAS** is Professor at *Sciences Po* University and Research Fellow with the *Centre National de la Recherche Scientifique*. She is a specialist of Russia at the *Centre d'Etudes et de Recherches Internationales* in Paris. She chairs the *Observatoire de la Russie*, a study group that produces original analysis presented at monthly seminars. Her publications deal with Russian political developments, questions of state-building and provincial rule, and Russian foreign policy. She is on the editorial board of the journals *Esprit, Le Courrier des Pays de l'Est* and *Konstitucionnoe obozrenie*, and contributes articles to the journals *Pouvoirs, Esprit, Commentaire*. Her most recent edited books are *Comment fonctionne la Russie ? Le politique, le* *bureaucrate et l'oligarque* (Paris, Autrement, 2003) and *La Russie de Poutine* (Paris, Le Seuil, « Pouvoirs », 2005).

Andrei **ZAKHAROV** is the Deputy Director of the Moscow School of Political Studies. In 1990 he was elected as a People's Deputy of the Russian Federation; from 1992 until 1993 he was a Member of the Supreme Council of the Russian Federation; and in 1993 he was elected to the Russian State Duma. From 1996 until 2004 he was the Vice President of the Foundation for the Development of Parliamentarism in Russia. Dr. Zakharov is the author of several books and articles dealing with the parliamentary practice, federalism, self-government and the development of civil society in Russia, including "Ein Novum mit Tradition: Föderalismus in Russland und Europa" in *Osteuropa*, 53, 9-10/2003, pp. 1469-1477; "Federalizm i globalizaciya" in: *Politicheskie issledovaniya*, 6/2002, pp. 116-126; and *E pluribus unum: ocherki sovremennogo federalizma* (Moskva, 2003).

About the editors

Katlijn **MALFLIET** is Professor and Director of the Institute for International and European Policy at the Catholic University of Leuven. She teaches courses on the political, social and legal transition process in Central and Eastern Europe. Since 2000 Katlijn Malfliet is the Holder of the Chair InBev – Baillet Latour on EU-Russia at KU Leuven. Her recent publications include "EU enlargement and the social function of property rights" in: Z. Mansfeldová, V. Sparschuh, & A. Wenninger (Eds.), *Patterns of Europeanisation in Central and Eastern Europe* (Hamburg, 2005: pp. 117-131). She co-edited with Francisca Scharpé *The Concept of Russia: Patterns for Political Development in the Russian Federation* (Leuven, 2003), and with Lien Verpoest *Russia and Europe in a Changing International Environment* (Leuven, 2001).

Ria **LAENEN** is a research fellow at the Institute for International and European Policy at the Catholic University of Leuven. Since 2004 she is the co-ordinator of the Chair InBev-Baillet Latour on EU-Russia at KU Leuven. Her research focuses on Russia's relations with the 'Near Abroad', ethnic minorities and the frozen conflicts in the CIS. She co-edited with Katlijn Malfliet *Minority Policy in Central and Eastern Europe: The Link Between Domestic Policy, Foreign Policy and European Integration* (Leuven,1998).

www.ingramcontent.com/pod-product-compliance
Lightning Source LLC
Chambersburg PA
CBHW052230230426
43666CB00034B/2588